POWER AND INFLUENCE

The Rules
Have Changed

POWER AND

INFLUENCE

The Rules
Have Changed

ROBERT L. DILENSCHNEIDER

MCGRAW-HILL

New York   Chicago   San Francisco
Lisbon   London   Madrid   Mexico City
Milan   New Delhi   San Juan   Seoul
Singapore   Sydney   Toronto

ISBN-13: 978-0-07-148978-8
ISBN-10: 0-07-148976-2

This publication is designed to provide accurate and authoritative information in regard to the subject matter covered. It is sold with the understanding that the publisher is not engaged in rendering legal, accounting, or other professional service. If legal advice or other expert assistance is required, the services of a competent professional person should be sought.

> —From a Declaration of Principles Jointly Adopted by a Committee of the American Bar Association and a Committee of Publishers and Associations

McGraw-Hill books are available at special discounts to use as premiums and sales promotions, or for use in corporate training programs. For more information, please write to the Director of Special Sales, Professional Publishing, McGraw-Hill, Two Penn Plaza, New York, NY 10121-2298. Or contact your local bookstore.

This book is printed on acid-free paper.

CONTENTS

To Jan,
who puts up
with it all

Acknowledgments

THIS BOOK FLOWS out of long decades of experience in the business world, and it would be impossible to thank everyone whose insights and perspectives contributed to my views on power and influence. In my earlier books, I have acknowledged my mentors and gurus, and key associates who offered ideas and provided intellectual stimulation over the years. My debt to them remains large and continuing.

In a very real sense, this book represents a synthesis of my thinking over the decades, limned by the developments of the recent past. It owes its birth to Herbert Schaffner, publisher of McGraw-Hill Professional, about whom I simply cannot say enough. I have followed Herb's sparkling career in American publishing with enormous interest, and with his ascension to the publisher's position at McGraw-Hill Professional in 2006, I felt that his talents had found ideal lodgings. Herb knows how the business world works, and his receptivity to the idea of this book was so immediate and warm that it would have been unthinkable for me not to have written it. I thank Herb profoundly for his encouragement, patience, and sharp editing skills.

At McGraw-Hill, Herb's boss, Philip Ruppel, Group Publisher and Vice President, also played a key role in making *Power and Influence: The Rules Have Changed* happen. I thank him, too, as I do Eileen Lamadore, Marketing Director; Tara Cibelli, Marketing Coordinator; Lydia Rinaldi, Publicity Director; and the McGraw-Hill sales and marketing team.

I have already acknowledged in this book's introduction the steady role of my longtime friend, the veteran author and journalist Pranay Gupte, in the development of "Power and Influence." I have rarely encountered a more obliging—or more cheerful—soul in the international media community. Pranay's career at *The New York Times*, Newsweek International, The Earth Times, and Forbes speaks for itself. But you will never catch Pranay himself speaking about his accomplishments. Perhaps it was his conservative upbringing in India, or perhaps it is the fact that he so focuses on listening to others, Pranay's modesty stands out in a media world too often characterized by self-promotion.

Modest, too, and self-effacing as well, is my longtime executive assistant, Joan Avagliano. Bluntly put, Joan not only is my right hand at The Dilenschneider Group, she is everyone else's. Her skills as an administrator and corporate executive are legendary in New York's business community. What is less known—but must be said here—is her ability to read people and to figure out intuitively their motives. Other than my wife Jan, there is no one whose judgment and instincts I trust more thoroughly. Joan's 24/7 dedication to The Dilenschneider Group contributes hugely to our business success; it also engenders the sort of good will that transforms clients and sometimes-even strangers into enduring friends and well-wishers. I felt compelled to include some of Joan's insights in this book; I have little doubt that one day she will write her own—and I sure hope that she will omit my surreptitious consumption of forbidden candy.

Laura Garrison, who also works directly with me as a member of my personal staff, exemplifies the kind of American whose enthusiasm and work habits know absolutely no bounds. From tending to my frenetic daily schedule to ministering to people whose calls can deplete anyone's patience, Laura is totally indispensable.

I wish I could name everyone at The Dilenschneider Group to whom I owe thanks in the creation of this book. But they know who they are, and I am, as always, grateful for their collegiality and cooperation.

But I'd be committing an unforgivable blunder if I did not mention Margarita Bravo, who transcribed endless hours of tapes of interviews conducted for *Power and Influence*.

I also wish I could name everyone who agreed to be interviewed for this book, for the record or off it. But it is a large list, and, in any case, the quotations are attributed to those I spoke to.

It is customary for an author to thank his immediate family for their patience and fortitude while he locked himself up in a garret in pursuit of the written word. Well, I did not quite lock myself up, but there were long periods when I wasn't available to be the doting dad to my sons Geoffrey and Peter. I won't speculate whether they missed me, but I certainly felt their absence, however much it flowed from my decision to be an author-in-isolation.

To merely thank my wife Jan for her contribution to this book would be completely inadequate. Her contribution has been vaster—to our marriage of nearly four decades. Not only has Jan raised two splendid sons, she has nourished my life in ways that have been unimaginably wonderful. Dedicating this book to her represents only a fraction of the payment on a lifelong—and humongous—debt that I owe Jan. She has truly powered and influenced my life and the lives of everyone who have ever come into contact with her.

Introduction

THIS BOOK IS about power—how to get it, use it, conserve it, keep it, and amplify it. You won't find the ideas, strategies, and tips in this book anywhere else.

I know about power. As an experienced corporate leader, I have wielded it. As an adviser to many of the most prominent chief executives and decision makers, I get to see on a daily basis how they wield their power. I know what it takes to get to the top—in corporate America, in philanthropy, in myriad fields around the world—and I understand the price of power in human terms. I've been there.

In this book, I will guide you toward gaining and wielding power in a warp-speed world that is being transformed by technology. In more than four decades in American and global business during which I have advised hundreds of companies, large and small, and individuals of considerable prominence, I have seen nothing like the relentlessness with which change is taking place in our country and almost everywhere else in this age of globalization.

Nothing is the same. Coping with that change—and leveraging it for benign purposes—is going to require the acquisition of power by individuals.

I will tell you how you can get the power to advance your interests in life and how you can get the power to make a difference in your profession. Ultimately, this book is about how, through acquiring the power and influence that you seek, you can have a positive impact on the society you inhabit.

This book therefore is about your future. In a larger sense it is also about how, by wielding personal power in a smart, techno-savvy, and ethical manner, you can help shape a more prosperous collective future for everyone.

In an age in which technological changes have spawned enormous anxiety for people in every walk of life, this book will be your guide regardless of where you live. This, after all, is an era of globalization in which borders are porous and ideas, capital, and people can cross frontiers more freely than ever before. If there's a connective tissue in all this, it is technology. Digital communications are affecting business, politics, economic growth, education, and, most fundamentally, the way people see their personal future.

There are few guidelines out there about how to survive and succeed in this emerging era of globalization.

This book offers universal principles that are informed by technological changes but speak to the verities of power and influence. The context is technological change, but the book is chiefly about your personal triumph. This book will not tell you how to live your life; it will offer guideposts that will enable you to live your life the way you want. For everyone, this means personal happiness, financial security, and professional success.

Most people do not understand power and what it can do for them. These individuals, often highly skilled and talented, are doomed never to live up to their potential and get all that is out there waiting for them. They suffer because of this. Their spouses or significant others suffer. Their children suffer, as do their friends and relatives. The suffering deepens as technological changes accelerate the demands of professional society.

In contrast, there are several accomplished men and women who have found the special key that unlocks the door to significant success in this age of bewildering globalization. By walking through that door, they are privy to a range of options and opportunities that most people would love to have. Of course, they do more—much more—than just walk through the door; they seize options and opportunities with canniness and vision. They have a plan for their lives and for their institutions. They generate velocity for their plans.

An old friend told me years ago that the world is populated with three types of people: those who make things happen, those who watch what happens, and those who wonder what happened.

There are many lessons to be learned from the successes I have seen. In this book, I will offer anecdotes and insights to illustrate the acquisition and amplification of power. You will read about well-known people I've encountered during my long career, and you will read about everyday people whose savvy and good sense enabled them to succeed. The most successful leaders I know don't get caught with their technological pants down in a warp-speed world.

In such a world, it doesn't matter how old you are; that is why this book is for all readers regardless of their age. If you are over thirty-five, the lessons in this book can help reenergize every phase of your life and make it more interesting and fulfilling. If you are under thirty-five, what you read here will strengthen your technological sophistication and vault you ahead of your peers.

You see, the game has changed dramatically. The rules of power and influence have been upended because of the technological revolution that has swept society globally. Technology has come of age in the process of gaining power and influence. Those who read this book and absorb and apply its prescriptions will learn how to use technology more effectively and succeed in their personal quest. In an increasingly competitive world, this book will arm you with the intellectual, technical, and moral weapons that you need to get ahead and stay ahead.

If there's an underlying goal for this book, it is that I want my readers to acquire happiness while they pursue material success. Henry David Thoreau said, "Most men lead lives of quiet desperation and go to the grave with the song still in them." I promise you that this book will guide you toward that special song in your heart; how you let the lyrics and cadences roll is up to you.

Personal happiness and professional power. It doesn't get much better than that.

My own lifelong quest for happiness and success has yielded a variety of dividends. I wrote this book partly to share those experiences.

In particular, I will share my and other people's experiences after the 2001 global recession. The tech revolution was in full swing, and too many of my clients, colleagues, and friends were not able to bounce back professionally as the U.S. economy began to pick up, as they had done before during other economic downturns. However, some did come back and were doing better than they had been in earlier years.

I asked myself, Why the difference?

Surely it wasn't age. One of those who came roaring back was the oldest of the baby boomers. Surely it wasn't just business experience. One man who was a big success in digital media had been a former pastor. Surely it wasn't gender. Men and women, including those of more ambiguous sexual orientations, all got stuck or were moving forward in equal proportions.

What made the question interesting and urgent was this: Rapidly my expertise in print media—the primary revenue generator for my international public affairs boutique, The Dilenschneider Group—was being challenged in the marketplace. What was growing in demand as tools of influence were the social media, that is, online chat rooms, bulletin boards, blogs, and podcasts, that were introduced early in the new millennium. I had little choice but to modify the way I did business.

Although top-tier print media such as *The Wall Street Journal* and *The New York Times* were not going to disappear anytime soon, they were no longer the only game in town or the media that offered the best and swiftest exposure for my clients. To remain a formidable player in communications, I knew that I had to get the edge in social media. I did just that—painfully. An extreme skills makeover was grueling. That is one reason why I have great compassion for readers who are facing major professional change.

To find out what I wanted to know about making a professional transition to an era of enhanced technology, I literally took to the streets. I interviewed, formally and informally, about a thousand winners in this flat-world economy. What did they have in common that empowered them to achieve success despite all the dizzying change surrounding them and their careers? My subjects ranged from teenagers to eighty-somethings.

I also interviewed the less successful. Why were they stuck? What would it take to get them unstuck? They ranged in age from the college years to seventy-something. It didn't take long to figure out that technology had changed everything about building, keeping, and adding to success.

I found out that some of the winners had had to "get it" the hard way: through a collapse of their industry, lay-offs, loss of their businesses, erosion of their brand names or reputation, lack of career mobility, being digitally ambushed, or just sensing that they were not players anymore. This technology shock was so overwhelming that most professionals couldn't ignore it, although some still do.

Here's one caution: Those who are casual about technology are likely to stay stuck in underemployment or unemployment.

A friend of mine, the veteran journalist and author Pranay Gupte, assisted with some of the interviews. He introduced me to valuable contacts, particularly in his native India and in the rapidly growing Indian-American community in the United States. It is only fair to cite Pranay's influence on this book.

When the research was completed, I ultimately arrived at ten principles for succeeding in a technology-driven volatile economy. I am convinced that by using these principles, readers who may see themselves as sidelined can make a comeback with new positions of strength.

In the following chapters I will elaborate on my principles, but in brief, here they are for your guidance:

- **Accept, adapt, and accelerate—or atrophy.** The professional world is changing. If your profession or industry has not been turned upside down yet, you can bet it's dying or soon will be. Denial of technological realities or failure to adapt to everyday technology may mean losing your job. Not only is technology ubiquitous, but we ignore it at our own peril because even white-collar professions have come to rely so much on it.

- **Be prepared to start over—again and again.** The challenge here is to do it and welcome doing it again and again. Attitude trumps résumé. A plethora of hard knocks improved Steve Jobs's attitude immensely, and look where he and the company he cofounded, Apple Computer, are now. His iPod has sold nearly 80 million units in five years. Now that Jobs has introduced the iPhone, a so-called smart phone that represents a synthesis of communications, music, video, and computers, he's poised to revolutionize telephony. Jobs changed the company's name to Apple, Inc., to signal that Apple would be moving beyond computers and moving more aggressively into consumer electronics; the potential for growth and profits seems limitless.

- **Think innovation—forget about just keeping up.** For executives and professionals, what counts is knowing enough about technical developments to determine a must-learn (e.g., learning how to explore the Internet productively). The merely technically skilled are making insignificant amounts of money, or their jobs are being outsourced to countries such as India and the Philippines, where labor costs are significantly lower than they are in the United States. Ironically, being a technical, or "pink-collar," professional in the digital age makes one's career less secure because those tasks increasingly are becoming commoditized. You will need to anticipate technological changes on the horizon or just beyond it. That means doing your homework painstakingly.

- **Seize the opportunity in every crisis.** The late management guru Peter Drucker wrote and spoke frequently in the early 1990s about turbulence as opportunity. What is new today is the scope and intensity of the turbulence. That means more opportunity. Examples of alert searchers include the blogger Ana Marie Cox, who is now a columnist for *Time* magazine; the enterprising gang at Google; spa owners; and toxic-tort attorneys.

- **Look beyond the new rules to connect.** Technology is transforming research, education (though some seem to be in denial), and financial services so rapidly that we don't know what the rules are at any specific time. The ability to capture attention is driving demand and growth. The growing demand is for whatever or whoever can capture attention, and that demand is setting the old media rules of decorum and low risk on their ear. Societies are being overloaded with information. Many of the old rules do not apply because information moves so fast that you become irrelevant professionally if you continue to do things the old-fashioned way. Information and opportunity exist in every corner of the globe. However, societies and systems consume technology differently, and so you need to be aware of cultural differences internationally.

- **Take the heat and never compromise.** The blogosphere and the freewheeling Internet chat forums that embrace virtually every subject under the sun have multiplied opportunities to escalate and sustain personal and professional attacks on people, particularly those who are prominent. What counts here is not the content or severity of the attacks but how one handles them. Precisely because the blogosphere has created an open, unfiltered megaphone for anyone with a computer and a modem, a striking characteristic of our times is unseemly incivility. Winners are never surprised by these assaults. You only have to talk for a few minutes to India's dynamic minister of commerce and industry, Kamal Nath, to get a sense of the fortitude it takes to survive more than three decades of electoral politics in a clangorous democracy like India, where it is a rare politician who doesn't get bruised.

- **Keep focusing on your strengths.** Often this means establishing one's own playing field(s). Until those positions are formulated, stay out of a game that's moving too fast for the fragile or the wounded. Almost any profession that one could think of is getting hypercompetitive. You need to take stock of your personal and professional assets and then build on them. Corporate executives need to understand that possessing strength, particularly in the corporate world, almost obliges you to empower others. Some of the shrewdest and most successful CEOs I know subtly convey to their colleagues their personal engagement with charitable giving. The acquisition and wielding of corporate power need not be confined to the precincts of a corporation; it can be used judiciously and generously in the cause of social justice, sustainable development, human rights, and protection of the environment, a subject that more and more businesses are embracing as part of the cause of corporate social responsibility.

- **Keep growing your network by shaving it.** Alliances are often temporary and shifting. Lopping off those which no longer are professionally useful can be a brutal process. Be prepared to trim your Rolodex. That does not mean that you should discard friends and associates precipitously. The plain truth is that in the corporate world you never know when careers will be resuscitated unexpectedly. By all means, stay in touch with everyone, but focus your special attention on those who are "players" in their fields and could be valuable allies.

- **Seek acclaim but practice humility.** In a flat, or decentralized, world there may be fewer and fewer superstars. However, that does not mean that you shouldn't seek and rightfully expect recognition and rewards for your effective enterprise. At the same time, it is important to maintain a core of humility. The best way to wield power is not to brag about it. Most notions of intellectual property are anachronisms. A red flag that someone is "pre–flat world" is an undue concern with copyrights and getting proper credit.

■ **Search for power but never forget to share it.** The new age of technology is all about sharing. The wielding of power must mean giving a helping hand to the dispossessed; it must mean leading the mannered life; it must mean thinking consciously about creating a personal legacy of fostering goodwill, funding good deeds, and furthering the aspirations of others. A boss or any professional who ruthlessly steps on others to climb the corporate hierarchy may well reach the summit, but he or she is not going to be respected.

These principles aren't abstractions, and this book isn't a fanciful cogitation on success. In the final analysis, it is a how-to book. It is meant to be read, savored, and reread.

This book will be your road map to success in a world where geography is less important than personal geopolitics, a world in which not a moment can be wasted ruing what might have been. It does not matter how far down you are in life; you can come back today, whereas in an earlier time you couldn't come back at all. The doors are opening wider. The issue is how do you get through the door? That is what this book is about.

There was a time when the doors weren't open. You were stymied by the social class structure, by income, by lack of education, by your inability to travel to centers of money and power. All that has changed. What you really need today is an idea, some courage, and the ability to project your idea. Once you understand how to project your idea and get an audience for it, how to expand that idea and make it a dramatic thing for the larger society, the possibilities are endless.

This is a book about those possibilities for power, success, and happiness. This is a book that declares in no uncertain terms that your time has come to gain power and apply it with wisdom to your own life and to the environment around you. Opportunities abound in an unprecedented way. You need look no farther than companies such as YouTube and MySpace.com, whose youthful founders reached out to vast constituencies of their peers, aggregated the interests of those young people, and created social networks that yielded billions of dollars in revenues for themselves.

There is one other thought I would like to share with you. I always have been interested in the interplay of faiths and in philosophy. I'm particularly struck by the works of one Zen master on the art of living. He says that the well-rounded professional makes little distinction between work and play, labor and leisure, the mind and the body, education and recreation, and love and religion. That person hardly knows which is which. This is an individual who simply pursues a personal vision of excellence in whatever he or she does, leaving others to decide if he or she is working or playing. To himself or herself, that person is always doing both.

That, to me, is leading the complete life. And now, as we say in the boardrooms of America, let us proceed toward a life of power, success, and, most of all, peace and happiness. Everything is changing, and you need to prepare for change.

1

Accept, Adapt,
and Accelerate — or Atrophy

To obtain and retain power, you have to create a
balance between your knowledge of technology and
your network of personal contacts and friendships.

WHENEVER I AM in New York, I eat at least
three or four times a week with a client at the Four Seasons,
the "21" Club, Lever House, Michael's, or another tony
restaurant celebrated for "power lunches." Those meals
are part of my job: I need to nurture and sustain professional relationships. Breaking bread with a longtime
client or a potential one at a classy eatery is always a fine
way to do business in a civilized, relaxed manner.

Did I say "relaxed"?

At those restaurants I increasingly see executives
hunched over their tables peering at their BlackBerries,
making cell phone calls, even though that often is not
allowed in those restaurants, or tapping their thumbs
on their PDAs to compose e-mail messages. In fact, at a
7 a.m. breakfast at the Palace Hotel in New York the other

day I spotted a man I knew well, a top Swiss businessman. On his left he was sending messages from his laptop, and on his right he had positioned himself with his BlackBerry, his cell phone, and his iPod to undertake other communications. He was doing all that with classic Swiss efficiency, but was he enjoying his collation, and what did his breakfast companion think about the host's heavily divided attention? The companion accepted the situation, took out his own cell phone, and made a call.

It was the waiter who took umbrage. A veteran of his profession, he stalked over and told both the Swiss executive and his companion that this just wasn't done in the public space of the hotel. The Swiss executive immediately left the table with his equipment and went to a stall for the handicapped in the men's room, where he continued working for about ten minutes before returning for breakfast.

All this is extraordinary. It would have been unimaginable five years ago, let alone ten, for executives to be multitasking over a multicourse meal. But the rules have changed, and they are changing even as you read this book. Just look around and gauge your daily experiences.

I used to receive thirty to forty letters a day. Now I get one or two and a ton of junk mail. Ten years ago I never thought of "logging on." Today I'm glued to some device or other that transmits my messages 24/7. Chief executive officers, the underpinning of my business model, used to be in their chairs for at least ten years; now their tenure is less than five years. There is a lot of speculation about why this is so: pressure from investors and Wall Street generally, board concern over litigation and corporate direction, and more. Frankly, I think one reason is that many CEOs did not grow up in a tech era and have not mastered the rapid movement that technology has created and with which one is forced to keep up.

On a recent flight from New York to Los Angeles, I observed eight people in the first-class cabin. One was sleeping, and another was watching a movie, but all the others were on their laptops or reading serious stuff. I'm pretty sure that some of the passengers were blogging. Alan Meckler, chairman and chief executive officer of JupiterMedia, an Internet media company in Darien, Connecticut, told the *San Jose Mercury News* that he views his corporate blog as a form of therapy. Imagine yourself at 40,000 feet, turning for succor to your computer instead of to libations.

Keeping up is a requisite for keeping your job and moving ahead.

Just the other day I got three e-mails from the Middle East and, two e-mails from Japan, and I talked to a friend of mine in Australia as well as to innumerable people all across the United States. That would not have happened ten years ago.

Ten years ago my daily mail would consist of personal letters sent to me by "snail mail"—the U.S. Postal Service. Now clients, colleagues, and complete strangers communicate with me by e-mail. People send thank-you notes by e-mail today. People send invitations by e-mail. I don't particularly like that, but it happens, and it is a bit of a change.

These days I am at risk or at a loss if I don't read certain blogs, such as those maintained by Mickey Kaus, Howard Kurtz (of the *Washington Post*), Arianna Huffington, and Andrew Sullivan, who provide keen insights on issues ranging from politics to business to media. I don't think anyone has an idea of the precise number of blogs out there, although Google's chief executive officer, Eric Schmidt, estimates that a blog is created every second. Thus the challenge for a blogger is to be able to break through, very much as a book has to break through the scrum of the more than 300,000 books that are published annually in the United States and just as a television show has to break through the intensifying competition among the networks and in the ubiquitous world of cable television.

Corporate chieftains have recognized the value of blogs. Michelle Quinn, writing not long ago in the *San Jose Mercury News*, characterized CEO blogs as follows: "Their writings are part strutting, part opining, part averting a train wreck by addressing criticism head-on. Sometimes executives share introspections of the late-night variety about the meaning of life and work.

"The duller ones have mastered the stiff and upbeat prose style of press releases, allowing no back talk from the riffraff and no mention of what they had for breakfast," Quinn continues. "The good ones—and yes, there are some—give a taste of life as a chief executive and engage their talkative audience, taking and throwing a punch along the way."

The demography of the world is also changing in a way that is sobering. More than 80 percent of the global population lives in the 135 developing—or poor—countries among the 192 members of the United Nations. That's more than 4 billion people out of a world population of some 6.4 billion. India's middle class of 400 million—out of an overall population of a billion-plus—is larger than the entire population of the United States. Europe's population steadily is becoming more nonwhite as African Muslims and other immigrants converge on countries like France, Germany, and Great Britain. And the United States? Well, the U.S. Bureau of the Census estimates that in another fifty years Hispanics will nearly constitute a majority of the population.

As the third world melds into the first world, people's aspirations for a better life keep rising. When Ted Turner transformed a sleepy southern television station into the global juggernaut of CNN, he could not have envisioned that in addition to broadcasting news on a twenty-four-hour basis around the world in real time, he would be spawning a whole new set of rising expectations. Little wonder that since the founding of CNN in 1980 the United States has been receiving and admitting a new wave of immigrants almost matching that of the early twentieth century. New immigrants see opportunities for economic and social mobility that may not exist in their homelands. The established organizations of civilian governance in the Western democracies offer a sense of security and stability to newcomers.

Everything is changing because social classes are breaking down in ways no one expected. Technology has contributed to this development because of its accessibility and availability. Opportunities are available for African Americans and Hispanics that weren't there twenty years ago, although not enough opportunities, of course. I recently talked to a man who is in the insurance industry, and I made the point that there are 300 million people in the United States, going to 400 million, and that most of the next hundred million are going to be Latinos. He said, "How do I begin to adjust my company, my policies, my promotion for Latino communication?"

That is something he wasn't really ready for. Thus integration has changed things markedly for young people. For them, technology has changed things, opening up a planet of possibilities. Ironically, the fact that the United States continues to be a melting pot has a lot to do with the creation of new opportunities for the young. The number of young south Asians, Filipinos, and Chinese who have contributed to the burgeoning and blossoming of technology industries throughout the United States is astounding. Taiwan-born Jerry Wang, for example, cofounded Yahoo!, which has become a global online community.

The language of technology is universal: You don't have to belong to any confessional faith to parse it. You only have to visit Google's campus in California or the offices of companies like Microsoft in Washington state to see how wonderfully men and women of dozens of nationalities and scores of different social backgrounds are able to work together. In technology, you only have to perform; the language you pray in does not count.

Technology also has become an "enabler" of sorts; that is, it's enabling various nations to develop closer economic and political relations. For example, implicit in President George W. Bush's overtures to Indian Prime Minister Manmohan Singh in 2005 was the recognition of Indian engineers' and programmers' contributions to Silicon Valley. Bush also recognized that India's increasingly open market has created a huge opportunity for American businesses, including those that produce technology hardware. The result? A bilateral strengthening of trade and diplomatic ties between the world's oldest democracy and its largest one.

As the digital age advances, the question of where one should establish one's home address or workplace becomes increasingly irrelevant. Today you may choose to live in California not just on account of Silicon Valley but also because it has that state's mostly glorious weather. Or you may choose to live in the historic city of Hyderabad in south-central India or in Dubai, one of the seven entities of the United Arab Emirates. But you don't necessarily have to work there. Technology enables everyone to telecommute. I know software programmers who live in Manila but whose headquarters are in Miami.

Technology is breaking down the myth that everybody in the world wants to live in the United States. A lot of people do, of course—the government hands out 300,000 immigrant visas each year—but a lot more are rediscovering their roots. For many people, in the final analysis, one's home culture and one's environment are far more comforting than the idea of transplantation to another society, even one as open and inviting as the United States. (Of course, in the wake of 9/11, immigration rules have been tightened, but the United States is still the most open society on earth.)

According to the U.S. Census, there are 2.3 million people of Indian origin in the United States today, and 200,000 of them are millionaires. Duke University researchers have estimated that 25 percent of technology and engineering companies that were started between 1995 and 2005 in the United States had at least a founder or a senior executive who was born outside this country. The same survey showed that companies started by immigrants to the United States employed nearly half a million workers and generated some $52 billion in revenue in 2005. Also, among the 7,300 technology start-ups founded by immigrants in 2005, 26 percent had Indian founders or chief executives. The Duke study also reported that Indian immigrants founded more technology start-ups in the last decade than did people from the next four largest sources of immigrations combined: Great Britain, China, Japan, and Taiwan.

These immigrants' success in technology has helped create a relatively new phenomenon: reverse immigration. I cannot begin to count the number of south Asians who have been in the United States and been educated here and then have gone back to India. Many have stayed in the United States, of course, and continue to maintain strong links to their native land. (The money that these "nonresident Indians—known by the acronym of NRI's—repatriate each year accounts for one of the biggest sources of foreign exchange for India—more than $25 billion.)

But many immigrants have gone back to apply their educational skills in their home countries. The same is true for the Japanese and now the Chinese. They are bringing an understanding of benign technology that they acquired in the United States to New Delhi, Karachi, Beijing, and various Asian places with mellifluous names. Then they fuse their new knowledge with the innate wisdom of their traditional societies and to economic foundations put in place through earlier development efforts. As a result, a highly exciting model of economic growth and social progress is being generated in many emerging countries. Indeed, if India sustains its current annual economic growth of 9 percent, it will become the world's third biggest economy in another twenty years, after the United States and China.

The returnees are telling their compatriots that you can change the social conditions and economic rules of your life faster than you thought possible. In some developing societies, people traditionally have held fatalistic views: "It's all in the stars," or, "I am destined to stay in my place." Those attitudes seem to be shifting these days. The returnees are saying to their brethren: "You can lift yourself up, and here is how to do it; I can lead the way." I think the two places where this has not taken hold fully yet are Africa, where tribal politics and massive governmental corruption still hold sway, and South America, which is controlled principally by established families that drive society fundamentally. But for the rest of the world, developed or developing, it is a huge change. I know we are going to see technology play a greater role in accelerating economic growth, political transparency, good governance, and social change.

One obvious factor is that people can watch television and see instantly what is happening. In London the other day, I saw on CNN a traffic jam in Los Angeles in real time. A friend in The Hague called me to comment on riots in the street in France. However, it is more than television. Who reading this book has not "Googled up" a person or a subject in the last week? If you haven't, it's time to do so because you will need information to plan your career. Who among us, preparing for a meeting with someone from outside this country, has not downloaded the relevant Web site? The list of possibilities grows.

The fashionable term for such change now is *globalization*. The process includes the freer flow of capital, ideas, goods, and services across increasingly porous borders. However, implicit in the notion of globalization is that in many societies some people are going to be left behind.

The challenge therefore is to empower those victimized by globalization, a point repeatedly emphasized in recent years by Joseph Stieglitz, the Columbia University economist and a recipient of the Nobel Prize for

Economics. Western society finally has awakened to the fact that there has to be an evenhandedness that didn't exist ten years ago, certainly not twenty years ago. We are all in the process of struggling to figure out a way for that evenhandedness to take place. That effort, unfortunately, has been compromised because there are still a lot of people who are prejudiced, a lot of people who don't understand: They are not smart enough to figure it out and absorb it. If they don't get it right, they are going to suffer significantly in the period ahead. That is another major change that has taken place.

Think about what has happened.

Consider the world of the arts and entertainment. Fifteen years ago there were three networks in broadcast television. Now I have access to 700 channels on my television set. Some of my neighbors in Connecticut, who subscribe to a different service, can get a thousand channels. The ability to get through those channels to figure out what one wants to see fractionates the audience dramatically. That is a huge change.

Take sports. Ten or fifteen years ago there were no multi-million-dollar athletes. Today the baseball player Alex Rodriguez—"A-Rod"—is making $25 million a year; the Yankees have an extraordinarily large payroll. It's just a matter of how much you want to spend to get the right team. (And even then, as Yankees owner George Steinbrenner has discovered, money does not necessarily buy championships.)

Fashion is another field where things have changed. It used to be that we had haute couture. You could go on the Rue St-Honoré in Paris and pick up a designer piece that would be one of only three pieces in the entire world. To a degree that is still true, but now Christian Dior, Yves

St. Laurent, and all the others merchandise their stuff in such a way that everybody can get it. Haute couture increasingly is giving way to the mass market.

Thus, the world of sports, the world of fashion, the world of media, the world of tolerance generally, and certainly the world of politics have all changed markedly over the last ten or fifteen years. And all this has been marked by e-mails, blogs, podcasts, teleconferences, and a dozen other ways to get a message out.

I think our society will undergo even more change that is going to be driven at the end of the day by the respective sensibilities of the haves and the have-nots. The have-nots are saying, "We're fed up," and they are tired and want to get something of their own. They are watching CNBC, Fox, and CNN, and they see that they are missing the "good life." For the most part, they are not happy.

It used to be that the haves could hold the line, but I think that is over now. I think it is just a matter of time before the have-nots adopt the spirit of the haves and get theirs. Smart entrepreneurs know that even a slight adjustment upward of a society's rate of job growth can translate into millions of new consumers. Throughout this book, I keep referring to India because it's a case study in progress of a society largely of have-nots that is being transformed energetically into a modern global giant. It already has the world's largest middle class at 400 million; another 400 million currently designated as poor are likely to join the middle class as India's economy continues to grow. Imagine: That's like adding another United States, Canada, and Great Britain combined to the cohort of the middle class. Imagine too how entrepreneurs must be salivating at the prospects of doing business there.

I believe that we are going to have to have a much more equal and balanced system in the near future. In a flattened world, information and technology networks have made billions of people aware of social and economic inequities. The influence, movement, consumer power, and sheer numbers of those global citizens will continue to accelerate the process of change. This will force each of us to think about our decisions in the context of a global order that is fairer to all.

How does this worldview of mine fit into this book's theme of power and influence? It is very simple: What happens "out there" deeply affects what happens "in here." That applies to individuals as much as it does to societies. It means that all of us need to accept change, adapt to it, and accelerate our efforts to accomplish the goals we set for ourselves.

Satchel Paige, the legendary pitcher for the Cleveland Indians, used to say, "Don't look back. Something might be gaining on you." Well, people are gaining on you today, and so it is time for you, regardless of your age and station in life, to step on the gas or be left behind as the world gallops past you.

More contemporaneously, Steve Forbes, chairman and editor in chief of *Forbes* magazine, sensed more than a decade ago that the business world would come to be dominated by technology. He calibrated the direction of his magazine in such a way that its coverage of technology and of the big players in the industry was well ahead of anyone else's.

It's very much like that at the Four Seasons restaurant in Manhattan, maybe the best watering hole in the world. The managing partners, the Italian-born Julian Niccolini and the Swiss-born Alex von Bidder, are very calm, organized, and relaxed about life. However, underneath there is a competitive streak in them because they realize that virtually every day people are coming up and trying to knock them off. They want to get the very best people into the Four Seasons—people who see and want to be seen—and they work overtime to do that. A lot of restaurants don't know how to do that, but Niccolini and von Bidder are excellent at it because they accept the growing competition, have adapted well to the exigencies of the age, and continually change the way their restaurant is run. They are unlikely to atrophy.

You need to do the same thing in your life.

I was introduced to the Four Seasons when I first came to New York in 1967. Not long after I'd joined Hill & Knowlton as an account executive, I met a woman named Lynn White. She was four feet eight inches tall. She was from Texas, had flaming red hair, and wore a big star on her dress that said, "Texas Ranger." And she was a character. I met her at a party, and Lynn White said, "Why don't you come over to the *Saturday Review* and meet a bunch of people over there like Goody Ace?"

I didn't know who Goody Ace was at the time, but I was later to learn. I also met George Lazarus, a marketing columnist, and John Ciardi, a literary writer and poet without parallel, among many others. They were the kind of people who were in New York at that time, and many were hard-core journalists. They were the kind of people you would go to lunch with, but they would end up sitting in a phone booth and having a martini served to them while they were making phone calls.

One day Lynn White said, "I want you to meet Norman." I did not know who Norman was. I wasn't smart enough. I hadn't done enough research, which is another power lesson, by the way: Do your homework. I had not done my homework. I said, "Norman?" She said, "Yes, Norman. Come on in."

I walked into Norman's office with some trepidation.

Norman, of course, was Norman Cousins, a legendary figure in publishing circles because of his acuity. He possessed high energy and an enormous supply of adrenaline. It was as though he had taken an upper; he was constantly in motion. But while that vitality kept flowing out, there was a marvelous elegance to him that characterized the kind of person he was. He was so smooth, so debonair; he had so much savoir faire. Everything about him said "power player."

Lynn White said to Cousins, "You are going to retain Bob Dilenschneider, and he is going to be our account executive."

Cousins said, "I don't have time for the small stuff; just go ahead and do it."

Then he said to me, "I want to get Cassius Clay in here to promote the magazine. Will you do it?"

"But how do I do this?" I said.

"I don't care how you do it, just get it done," Cousins said.

Fortunately, that wasn't the end of my association with the *Saturday Review*, and we would come up with things that would result in promoting the magazine. It was a great literary magazine. Unfortunately, it failed because things literary often fail. That was what happened to it. It was for people who cared about ideas and about thinking. The people at the magazine were terrific. They would sit in small offices—cubbyholes—and almost anything was possible. The concept of the dream was really there. These were people who had dreams, ideas, and visions, and they made their dreams, ideas, and visions come to life on the printed page.

They hosted literary parties at the *Saturday Review* office or at places like the Century Association. The *Saturday Review* guys would hold forth, and people would come from *Harper's*, from *The Atlantic*, from the *New York Review of Books*.

It was a fascinating world. In many ways I regret the fact that I am now in much more of a staid world—the world of business—because it was a lot more fun back in those days. I think that is another principle I learned along the way: It is important to have fun. If you are miserable at your job, even if it potentially could be exciting, if you don't have some fun along the way, that job is not worth a lot.

I also learned in those days that it is important to give back and add value to your environment. The people at the *Saturday Review* probably could have made a lot more money doing something else in some other walk of life, but they didn't choose to do that. They chose to write their columns, compose their articles—whatever it took. It was quite an experience. Their view was "Give it back." That meant sharing their passion and romance with their audience.

I learned other lessons from them too. One staff reporter said, "When you work here, people try to pull the wool over your eyes all the time. Don't ever let them do that. Keep asking questions until you get to the core truth. Once you get to the core truth, keep asking more questions." It was very smart instruction in how to use the power of inquiry to keep from being fooled.

These are lessons and messages that I've kept with me for my whole life in terms of how to conduct myself.

My experience with Norman Cousins helped mark my life in many ways. I admired his work and energy. However, I also noted that he had a certain style and a way of handling himself that left a deep impression that I still carry with me.

Three or four times a week in the late 1960s and early 1970s, Cousins and I, along with Lynn White, would have lunch at the Four Seasons. Cousins would sit there for two, three, and sometimes four hours, savoring the food but not drinking and, in his own fashion, entertaining New York's great, greatest, and near great at his table. People like broadcaster Walter Cronkite, and *New York Times* drama critic Walter Kerr would come to the table. They would sit down and engage in a conversation with Cousins. It was like having a literary salon at the restaurant.

Cousins treated me almost like a mascot; I in turn treated those lunch sessions as a great way of learning the trade. We talked about everything. We talked about Georgia O'Keeffe; we talked about New York City politics; we talked about people like Mayor Edward Koch and Mayor Abraham Beame, who would come by. I remember that Morley Safer came by one time. All those notables would sit there with Cousins, and they would talk about Jack Kennedy, about Richard Nixon, about Lyndon Johnson, about Konrad Adenauer, West Germany's first chancellor in the postwar era; they'd talk about Indira Gandhi of India. They would talk about the whole range of things that were taking place in the world.

What Cousins was doing in those years was exposing me to two things: one was the world of ideas and ideas of the world, and I previously had had little exposure to those eclectic ideas. After all, I was from a small town in Ohio, and I tended to be parochial in nature.

The second thing was that Cousins showed me a way to handle other people with ease and respect and sophistication. I can never imagine or recall Cousins in those days insulting anybody. It just did not happen. If Cousins was insulted, he took it with a smile and thanked the person for the comment. Thus, he taught me a whole way of social behavior; he transformed my Midwestern way of operating into something as sophisticated as I was able to be.

They were really lessons in the use of power. The subtext of those lessons was that the "old rules" of good manners and ethical behavior never truly get old. To that I would add that the enduring old rules should be incorporated into the new rules of our more tempestuous times.

Cousins taught me, for example, how to handle anger. He said, "When you get really angry, just wait a while, a couple of hours; wait a day. Your reaction after you get really angry will be very different then from what it is immediately." He was right, and I've done that ever since.

He taught me about civility. Cousins said, "When you are in the presence of people, there is no need to curse. You don't have to curse." He used a quote from G. K. Chesterton in which the great English essayist and humorist said that you don't have to curse to get your point across; in fact, if you don't curse and you use language elegantly, it is much more effective than cursing. ("I regret that I have no gloomy and savage father to offer to the public gaze as the true cause of all my tragic heritage," Chesterton, a devout Roman Catholic, wrote of his beginnings, "and that I cannot do my duty as a true modern, by cursing everybody who made me whatever I am.")

Cousins taught me how to order lunch, and he would admonish me about overeating. He talked about how certain wines go with meals. He talked about how to be very courteous to the waiter, because the waiter is more important than the owner of the restaurant. The owner of the restaurant is there to seat you and take your money. The waiter is there to handle your experience while you are dining.

He taught me how to listen when people would come to the table and to ask questions and draw them out instead of telling them my story. Don't get me wrong. Norman Cousins had a big ego; he was not a man unimpressed by his own persona. But he was a marvelous listener, and that is an important characteristic of a power player.

"Everybody has a story to tell; just listen to the story," Cousins told me. "If you hear the story, you'll hear things along the way and ask people about those things, and they will tell you more. What will come your way are a richness of life and a richness of experience, and you will be better off for it. And the person will like you for having asked you about their story."

My relationship with Cousins continued for three or four years. It was a priceless education at the table of a peerless master. Mentorship is essential, especially in an age when corporations have become juggernauts where junior executives can go unnoticed for years unless they have a senior person championing their cause in-house.

There's a perception that those who work in technology blithely float toward fortunes, that mentorship is not needed. However, if you look at many of those who have succeeded, such as Larry Page and Sergey Brin, the founders of Google, they invariably turned to mentors to guide them during the critical first stages of their new enterprises. (As you will see later in this book, some mentors even invest their own money in a new project.

The Google duo's early benefactor was a venture capitalist in Silicon Valley, Ram Shriram.)

"I call this 'mentor technology,'" says Kris Ramanathan, a cofounder of Netomat, Inc., a technology start-up based in New York. "Regardless of how much you know about technology and about applying it in your personal pursuit of success and power, you have to get others onboard. So you need someone credible to get others to imagine your value—and values—in their mind. A good mentor will do that."

The concept of mentorship isn't new, but perhaps it's a little more formalized these days. During the Cousins era a powerful man just "adopted" you, and if you were smart about figuring out things, you quickly realized how fortunate you were.

Of course, the Cousins era was a very different time. Money mattered, but ideas and friendship counted more. It was an easier time. The pace was not as fast. More deliberation went into discussions. Conversations wandered into history and ideas far more than they do today.

We may never return to anything close to that era. It was a time to stop and admire a painting or a scene from nature. Just the other day I was driving on a golf cart through Tucker's Point in Bermuda, one of the most beautiful bits of land in the world. The rich features, the flora, and the picturesque surroundings were spectacular, but I had to leave to catch a plane and needed to do my e-mail before getting on it. Could I have stayed at Tucker's Point? Yes, and maybe I should have.

People at the Four Seasons are listening to one another all the time, surreptitiously, of course. They are not listening in a positive way to what is being said at the next table. They are listening to extract information. People are watching who is sitting with whom and where, and they are commenting on who is sitting with whom, when, and where. With Norman Cousins, people would come up to the table, very relaxed, and no one made a big thing of it. Nowadays everyone wants to know who you are sitting with.

Nowadays IPOs, private equity, and hedge funds dominate the discussion, not ideas. The coin of the realm seems to be the size of one's annual bonus. Professional success with a company's bottom line, more than moral leadership, seems to be the way to assess a CEO's ability.

Technology dominates every moment of our lives and shapes our conversations as much as our thoughts. (I often wonder if people converse in complete sentences any longer. Buzzwords like *cool* often serve to convey an entire attitude or mindset. And how about *chill?* The reference is rarely to the weather.)

My point is that the whole social construct and its economic edifice have changed. Nevertheless, the old rules I learned under Cousins, which I apply even today, still can help you become successful. Also, there are new rules you need to know that are driven by the times and by technology.

Today you have to be very careful, very guarded. You have to think about things well in advance of doing them because you don't want to make a mistake. Thus, the day of the Cousins lunch unfortunately has passed.

As with Norman Cousins, I have been fortunate to meet people who were visionary and who had foresight.

For example, when I started The Dilenschneider Group in 1991, Richard Mahoney and Robert L. Berra, then the two top executives at Monsanto, warned me, "Be flexible and adapt to the changes around you . . . with what is happening. Be vigilant, and if you can, lead the change."

That was great advice, and I owe those two men a great debt.

The fact is, I have found totally new ways of communicating and moving others to take action. For instance, I know when to send "snail mail" because it will get attention. For example, Otto Penzler, a celebrated publisher of crime novels, wrote me this note about a letter I sent about his published appreciation when the crime novelist Mickey Spillane died:

> Dear Mr. Dilenschneider: Many thanks for your gracious note about my tribute to Mickey Spillane. Clearly, this wonderful man struck a chord with a great number of people, as I had more than 120 e-mail messages within three days after the piece ran—every one of them positive. Yours, however, was the only one I received the old-fashioned way, on a piece of paper with a signature, and thus it resonated ever more strongly. It was kind and thoughtful of you to write, and I am truly appreciative.

Although I take care to send handwritten notes when that is warranted, I also have learned how to use e-mail, blast faxes, and employ iPods. This is technology that some people—in fact, many people in my space—are still struggling with. Was it hard? It was difficult at first, but it got easy once I applied myself and once the makers of the equipment made it simpler.

What I found hard was setting the parameters of where to use technology. For example, I try to answer every e-mail I receive within twenty-four hours. Why? To keep a dialogue going. That is what life and business are all about today: sustained dialogue.

I work with two men who are big hitters in their companies. When I'm in their offices, I see that the screens on their PCs are clogged with e-mails. I ask each how many they receive a day. They say 300 to 400. I ask if they respond to them. They say no, they do not have the time. Imagine what the senders of those e-mails must think when no reply is forthcoming.

On certain occasions throughout the year—Labor Day, Thanksgiving, and the Christmas holidays—I send by "blast e-mail" a personal message that I've researched about those moments. It always strikes a responsive chord with hundreds of recipients. My goal is to give back, to help people remember what those moments mean, and to let them know that I am there with them.

Whether it's by fax, e-mail, or mass mailings, people appreciate it when you stay in touch with them and share special thoughts. It isn't hard to do this; it's actually fun, and it's rewarding. You need to figure out how to customize this technology for yourself.

You must see technology as only an enabler. It's not a substitute for clear thinking. A BlackBerry or Treo makes it possible to communicate instantly with someone 10,000 miles away, but your message has to be clear for it to make sense. This may seem a no-brainer, but you'd be surprised how many confused messages one receives during the course of a business day.

That is why I emphasize the importance of logic, good thinking and solid reasoning, and decent writing: No matter how skilled you become with technology, the basics of forming, parsing, and punctuating your argument have not changed. You still need to communicate your thoughts sensibly and pithily. Throwing volumes of information into your correspondence does not make you more effective unless your note is well organized.

That is why I was delighted to see a secondary school in my Connecticut neighborhood double the number of teachers delivering a course in Latin, which offers rigorous discipline in sentence construction.

At my alma mater, Notre Dame, I sponsor a lecture series on the evolution of religion and the classics. In my son's high school in Connecticut, my son takes several accelerated history courses. I firmly believe that young people must understand history and its lessons. Without it they have no or little grounding for their future.

With all the technology out there, I try to read eleven newspapers every weekday and six on the weekend, read at least two books a week, and constantly listen to and watch the news: CNBC is turned on right next to my desk, and Fox and CNN are steps away. I realize that not everyone has the ability to monitor the media that intensively; I do it because I'm in the communications business. But if not every business channel or publication, I would urge readers to look at *The Economist* and *The New Yorker* each week and follow some of the programs on the Public Broadcasting System (PBS), especially anything produced by Bill Moyers.

Why is all this important? It teaches us how to think, how to organize, how to express an argument, and how to observe the world as it evolves around us.

Can you do it? Of course, so get out and nurture your relationships; do not wait for life to happen for you. Know when to use snail mail. Answer every e-mail within twenty-four hours. Identify the blogs you must read and read them every day. No matter what device you use to communicate, make your arguments thoughtful and logical. Think about the big drivers of life—politics, business, arts and entertainment, sports, fashion—and how you can play a role. Deepen your level of tolerance for the social change that is gripping the world. Listen to other people, and then listen some more. Be relentless but have some fun—and do it with style.

2

Be Prepared to Start Over—Again and Again

Attitude trumps résumé.

YOU MUST BE ready to fight again even if you've been knocked over or knocked out.

Be careful: Power and influence are transitory and elusive. I know many men and women who had power only to see it slip from their grasp.

Former CEOs, people who lost money in the market, executives forced into retirement or pushed out in buyouts and their spouses, journalists, and security analysts who were at their posts but were fired during cost reductions—these were all people who once had it and then lost it and did not know how to recover.

At a recent dinner party I sat next to the wife of a CEO who was about to retire. She told everyone how important she was, whom she had been with, when she was going on holiday, and more. No one cared. Why? Because she merely *told* us her story and did not bother to *engage* us sufficiently. She was accustomed to having people hang on her every word.

When you have power, you have to know how quickly you can lose it and know what to do about that. I have long admired Steve Jobs, the cofounder of Apple Computer. He started the company with his friend Steve Wozniak in the proverbial garage in California. He built up Apple, only to be fired by his own board of directors, mostly because of corporate politics. What did Jobs do? He started another company, Pixar, which specializes in animation and has become dominant in the industry. Eventually, as Apple foundered under the stewardship of Jobs's successors, the board invited him back as chief executive. What happened then? Jobs invented the iPod and other hugely successful products. In effect, he remade Apple even as he remade himself, successfully battling cancer along the way.

Steve Jobs was prepared to start over at Pixar, and he was ready to start over again at Apple upon his return. He never lost his vision. He never lost his drive. He never let power go to his head. Steve Jobs is a real power player, and real power players have resilience. Early in 2007 Jobs showed that he still had a few tricks up his sleeve. He conjured up the iPhone, a smarter than smart phone that does practically everything a consumer wants other than brew coffee. Jobs was among the first entrepreneurs to understand the convergence of communications, computers, telephony, and video.

Power players like Jobs know how to come back. They never tell us in so many words. They *engage* us and permit us to celebrate their success with them. They are generous people.

They understand that not everything is going to work. They find a way to make a comeback after a professional defeat. There are many examples of people who have been humiliated on the Broadway stage and have come back by reinventing themselves. People in movies come back and do it differently. Singers reemerge. Neil Diamond, Tony Bennett, and Elton John are sterling examples of resilience. How do they do it? They simply say, "We are determined to use our talent to rise to a higher level. We are not going to let this failure diminish us."

Comebacks happen in politics too. An intemperate Richard Nixon famously announced to the media after he lost the California gubernatorial race in 1962—after he'd already lost the 1960 presidential campaign to John Fitzgerald Kennedy—that they wouldn't have him around to kick anymore. But six years later Nixon was back as the thirty-seventh president of the United States after defeating Democrat Hubert Horatio Humphrey in a close race. Al Gore, the former vice president of the United States and a defeated candidate for president, is making a comeback by using global warming as a platform. His film on global warming, *An Inconvenient Truth,* recently won an Oscar for best documentary.

In this age of corporate downsizing, mergers, out-sourcing, layoffs, and mass dismissals, you are going to have to come to terms with the fact that there is little job security. Even though corporate profits rarely have been higher and even though the U.S. gross domestic product is surging past $13 trillion, companies are taking their cue from Wall Street: Streamline expenses, cut the workforce, make even higher profits for shareholders.

In short, the era of the paternal corporation that took care of people from cradle to crypt is over. Many studies show that a typical professional in this early part of the new millennium will need to change jobs six or seven times. That means that you have to be prepared to start over again and again.

On the face of it, that may seem daunting. Anyone who's been fired knows how terrifying it is to be stripped suddenly of job security, not to mention a regular income. Foreclosures suddenly stare you in the face. Health insurance is gone. There's the social embarrassment of being canned from one's job. Marriages sometimes unravel as economic circumstances worsen.

This is where technology can be your ally. Look at the proliferation of Web sites such as Monster.com and craigslist.org. They are rich resources for information about what's available in the job market. Indeed, more and more newspapers that traditionally viewed classified ads as cash cows are seeing their clients drift to the Web. No wonder an increasing number of publications are making deals with online services such as Yahoo! to share classified ads and, of course, the revenues from those ads. Even executive search companies scour the Web to spot candidates for top-level jobs. Technology has become an ally of corporate America's human resources departments.

My point is not that obtaining a new job after losing the previous one is getting easier. I'm saying that technology has widened the resources available for job seekers. The Web offers extraordinary details to the job seeker: not only the types of jobs available but locations and even neighborhoods within cities. Full-time, part-time, temporary gigs—you name it. That proverbial bulletin board at the local laundry or grocery store has gone digital. You can summon up job opportunities anywhere in the world on your PDA.

Be advised, however, that you are unlikely ever to graduate from the school of hard knocks.

Like Steve Jobs, I attend the school of hard knocks. Many years ago in Chicago, I remember being told that my public relations company had gotten the Sears Roebuck account. My colleagues and I went out dancing that night, only to learn the next day that we hadn't won the account after all. It was absolutely devastating to learn that. I had told all our employees that we had it, had told my boss that we had it—and we didn't get it. Even though it was an embarrassment and a setback for me professionally, I said to myself that the sun was going to rise the next morning and that I'd better prepare for another day.

I grew up in Ohio always thinking that tomorrow was going to be a better day and knowing that I could influence the day. Over the course of my life, I've decided on the three or four things I want to get done each day. The night before, I write out a small list to myself, and then, when I get up, I work on those three or four things. Do I get everything done? Not always, but I do focus on the things that I've prioritized, and I feel that by doing that I'm moving things forward.

Of course, I know that I have the luxury of a car and driver so that I can work while being transported from one appointment to another. With a BlackBerry at my disposal, the machine alerts me to all my appointments and chores. If traffic prevents me from reaching a destination in time, I can send a text message alerting my host that I may be late. People appreciate these courtesies. I surf the Web in my car to look for details about my prospective customer. I write memos and letters on my PDA that I instantly beam to the office so that my staff will have them printed out by the time I return to the office. Technology and I work hand in hand.

That does not mean that I expect life to go totally smoothly. I'm experienced enough to know that regardless of one's attention to planning and research, setbacks are bound to occur. That's simply part of the scheme of things. However, I've learned that when setbacks occur, you have to bounce back. You also must learn the lessons from the setbacks.

Whenever I have a setback—and I've had dozens—I say to myself, "What can I learn from this problem? What can I learn from this humiliation? What can I learn from this embarrassment? What can I learn from this loss?"

Sometimes on a piece of paper, but these days mostly on my BlackBerry or computer, I put down two or three things that were fundamental to the loss or the embarrassment. Frequently it comes down to one thing: It all happened because of a judgment issue. It's been said that judgment is intuitive, but judgment also flows from keen observation and analysis. Good judgment requires reliable facts.

If your judgment fails you and you end up making a mistake, it's natural to be upset. I've gotten mad an embarrassing number of times after setbacks, sometimes blaming associates when the fault lay squarely with me. I'm the boss, and the buck stops at my desk; it's not wise for me to point fingers at someone else, however blameworthy he or she may be. It's even less wise for me to forget a lesson that my father, a newspaperman, taught me many years ago: Just forget about it for several hours, and your outlook on that situation will change.

This is an important lesson when it comes to making a comeback. People will remember you for your tirades and tendency to blame others. Some people I know will meditate during times of crisis. Now technology has come to the rescue. Why not surf the Web at moments of stress? You'd be surprised how calming that can be.

You might ask, What does it take to make a comeback, to start all over again? Does it take nerve? Does it take special smarts?

It certainly takes nerve because once you have been brought to your knees, you say to yourself, "God, do I really want to do this again?" It also takes smarts. It takes the ability to figure out what your next move is going to be. It takes application and technology. I think that in today's modern world, if you don't rely on technology to do what you need to do to come back, you won't have much of a chance. Technology, in the form of research services such as Lexis-Nexis, among others, can arm you with facts and figures that will strengthen your candidacy for the next job.

Coming back is not easy. I always advise people who are trying to put their lives back together to focus on a very few things that they want to do. Say to yourself: "I really want to feel good about myself." Focus very hard on doing that, and it will help you overcome the problems that stem from the humiliation. The humiliation usually hurts at least as much as the reversal in economic fortunes.

When people lose jobs or have to change careers, they often feel a lack of worth. Once an organization has fired them and humiliated them and humbled them, it doesn't care about them at all. The best thing to do is erase that organization from your memory. Just forget about it because it never is going to help you again. That is not to say that you should jettison valued personal relationships that transcend the workplace. You may find that some of those friendships can give you a boost in the next phase of your career.

Often people say they want to strike out: "I want to get Johnny" or "I want to get Company X." This is a big mistake. Company X and Johnny do not care about you, so why should you care about them? Keep going. Develop a new network. Find a new set of friends. Reach out to people who not only will help you but whom you can help. Be a giving person. Remember Kris Ramanathan's dictum of mentor technology. Those are important things.

I realized the importance of moving on mentally and emotionally when I left Hill & Knowlton, where I had been a successful CEO. I said to myself, "What do I really want to do now?" Answering that question required a step-by-step approach, rebuilding a reputation and a business to what The Dilenschneider Group is today. There were many steps along the way where people wanted to knock me off or wanted to see me as not successful, but I was determined to try to do it.

Why was I so determined to start over? I think the reasons are very simple. First, I wanted to earn an income for my family and myself. Second, I said to myself, "I want a fulfilling life." Third, I saw the possibility of making a contribution to a greater whole: American society. I thought that was really important. I never had in my mind the idea that I had to show people who didn't think I was going to be successful that I was going to be successful. Their approval didn't matter.

How was it that I, a successful CEO at one of the world's largest communications companies, found myself one sunny September afternoon stepping out of the Four Seasons and walking up thirty-five blocks on Park Avenue to my Fifth Avenue apartment to tell my wife, Jan, that I no longer had a job? My story probably mirrors that of thousands of other executives who find themselves unemployed and need to prepare themselves to start over.

I had worked for twenty-five years at Hill & Knowlton, a company of top-quality professionals. I was an administrator of 4,000 people, overseeing eighty-six offices not only across the United States but in far-flung places such as Australia, China, and Malaysia. I oversaw balance sheets. I assessed company strategies. I would hop aboard flights to Hong Kong to meet with Jardines or Hutchinson Whampoa or to London to see Sir John Bond or to Florida to advise giants like J. Peter Grace about their business development.

Hill & Knowlton was acquired by J. Walter Thompson (JWT). The new management made all kinds of promises about how we were going to have autonomy. Of course, everything changed immediately. Our company was transformed quickly into a rules-dominated bureaucracy whose prime function seemed to be to develop paperwork that had little to do with the production of results for our clients. The people at J. Walter Thompson were good at advertising; they could put together a great program for Kellogg's or Unilever. However, they didn't really understand anything beyond selling goods and services. JWT, which was full of great people, didn't understand the nature of public opinion. They didn't understand the nature of power. They didn't really understand how life worked around the world. Hill & Knowlton did something very different. We communicated and sold ideas, a point of view, and that was a kind of a paradigm that JWT didn't understand. I spent a lot of time writing memorandums, refereeing meetings, and sitting with people saying that John didn't mean that and Jerry didn't mean this. It was all counterproductive.

Then J. Walter Thompson was taken over by WPP. That British company is the largest marketing services company in the world today. Its founder, Sir Martin Sorrell, is a very numbers-oriented guy, and everything was done by the book. His team would meet with me once a month. They would come in carrying huge books under their arms. The books were full of numbers, and we'd sit down at the end of the table in the conference room. They would ask questions like, "Why does the guy in Kuala Lumpur have a subscription to *Time* magazine?" I thought it was absurd. There were escalating efforts to get rid of good people at Hill & Knowlton, and so I made the decision to leave Hill & Knowlton. I hired a lawyer from Sidley & Austin to ensure that I would have the ability to do business once I got out of Hill & Knowlton. Sir Martin was the kind of guy who, if he had a hold on you, would exercise that hold.

It took me over a year, but it worked, and one day I was finally free.

In my first moment of freedom I thought of a lesson that Andrew Chancellor had taught me many years before. Chancellor was a guy I had grown up with at Hill & Knowlton. He had been an editorial writer for the *Pittsburgh Post-Gazette*. He is probably one of the smartest people I have ever met. Andy could recite the names of all the kings and queens of England; he knew Greek and Latin; he was trying to study Sanskrit so that he could figure out how to deal with India's ancient culture. Andy always said, "Be your own person. Don't let the organization ever surround you and beat you down."

On leaving Hill & Knowlton, my wife asked, "So what are you going to do?"

"I think what I'll do is call a few people I used to do business with and see if they want to work with me," I said.

I called a man named Wright Elliott at the Chase Manhattan Bank and Tom Lebrecque, who at that time was the bank's CEO. They invited me for lunch the next day and became clients. I called J. P. Bolduc and J. Peter Grace at W. R. Grace, and they became clients immediately. I called Bob Diamond of Dun & Bradstreet, and he became a client immediately. I called three or four other chief executives I'd known over the years. They all became clients immediately, and that was how I started over.

I turned to the old rules that had served me well: I figured out a way to serve those people and bring them value for what they were going to pay me. I found that the value really wasn't in bricks and mortar or in developing press releases and hawking them to *The New York Times* or *The Wall Street Journal*. The value was in thinking things through and helping them cope strategically with their business problems. This approach has been at the core of my company since I launched it seventeen years ago.

The old rules easily translated into the new rules. Clients cared about the quality of service they got, and I was offering continuity from the past to the present.

I had the advantage of having created a large network of people at Hill & Knowlton; those top executives really didn't care about the imprimatur of Hill & Knowlton. They cared about what I was able to bring to the party. That is what made the difference. I was quick to realize that if I let them down for a second, it would be all over, and so I had to continue to produce at a high level, in fact, higher than before. Whenever someone would ask me to do something, I would do that, but I always asked myself, "How can I do more? Not only for money, but how can I do it better, and how can I provide something that this client isn't getting and can't get anywhere else?" It was a matter of mentally and emotionally stretching myself for a client, and it has worked out very well.

Another lesson that I learned in starting over was that you have to bet on yourself. That lesson was taught to me by Ray Chambers, who, with former Treasury Secretary William E. Simon, had formed one of the original buyout firms. Chambers offered to lend me $350,000, which I declined because the terms that his aide, Kurt Borowsky, tried to set were far too onerous. But Chambers then did something even better than lending me money: He started sending business my way.

So did the famous economist Henry Kaufman. So did John Gutfreund, then the head of Salomon Brothers.

As it happened, Gutfreund found himself out of a job—a fate he did not deserve—after a corporate scandal at his Wall Street company, a precursor of the woes that were to afflict the financial services sector in subsequent years. He took the fall when in truth others were much more culpable. An underling had cooked the books, but as Michael Bloomberg, who had worked for Gutfreund at Salomon Brothers and was fired by him well before the corporate scandal, wrote in his autobiography, Gutfreund had become an icon of the corporate excesses of the 1980s. He found himself without the money, the power, and the influence. Gutfreund found himself having to start all over again.

He did that by discovering the things that really mattered and made a difference to him: his intellect, his humanity, his compassion for other people, and his ability to laugh and tell jokes. I think he enjoys his life more now. He goes to ball games at Yankee Stadium and sits in the stands like everyone else: No more skyboxes for him, no more retinues of flunkies making way for him as he moves about in search of a hot dog.

You'd think that Gutfreund would be embittered, but he's blessed with loads of friends, including Mike Bloomberg, who went on to launch a successful technology and communications company and later became New York's mayor. Everyone wants him at his or her party or seeks his advice. There's a lesson in this for people who need to start over: Keep your friendships, nurture them, and don't expect anything in return. At the same time, when someone else has a problem, help that person instead of shying away from him or her. Most people tend to look at people with problems and say, "I want to avoid those people." The time to go to people is when they're down and out. They are unlikely ever to forget your goodwill.

I know that I will never forget a touching gesture by Rabbi Arthur Schneier of the Park East Synagogue in Manhattan. He called me shortly after my exit from Hill & Knowlton to invite me, a Roman Catholic, to his temple.

"I'm going to say a prayer for you," Rabbi Schneier said. Then he gave me a pat on the back and added: "You are going to be fine. If I can help, let me do it."

That prayer session with the rabbi was inspiring and gave me a special kind of hope. It brought home to me the notion that the United States is a country of second acts. Much later, I thought about another major corporate player, Brigadier General Robert Francis McDermott, who after retiring from the U.S. Air Force joined the United Services Automobile Association (USAA). He made it the country's largest provider of insurance products to military members and their families. However, as is inevitable in the corporate world, McDermott had to retire from his second act.

He moved on to a third act, starting all over again. This time he dedicated himself to developing theme parks and assisting not-for-profit organizations in San Antonio, Texas. He created programs for the treatment of drug abuse and alcoholism. He established computer networks linking the various charitable organizations that he helped. The general, raised in another age, became tech-savvy.

My friend Jane Genova is another start-all-over-again example, one whose latest reincarnation is that of a blogger. Indeed, she's become one of the country's most successful bloggers (www.janegenova.com). She holds an MBA from Harvard and has a long list of corporate accomplishments, including speechwriting and ghosting books.

I happened to be discussing this book one day with Genova when word arrived that Donald Rumsfeld had just resigned as defense secretary.

"Today Rumsfeld is just another unemployed geezer," Genova said. "We geezers who've been there—out of work and out of luck—know exactly what he has to do now if he wants to work again. In fact, Geezerville is full of anecdotes about those of us who suffered horrific professional reversals and managed not only to land on our feet but to be better positioned than before."

During our conversation, Genova told me that she had devised a plan that she called the Seven Steps of Geezer Work. Among those steps, Genova said, is the need to incorporate frugality into one's life. Professionals of a certain age who find themselves bereft of a job should treat the situation as a "bottom," Genova said. They should "ask for help—selectively." They should "get over aging" and look for employment in areas where age discrimination won't be an issue.

"At the age of fifty-eight, I snagged two great survival jobs by selling myself so aggressively that there was no space for age to emerge in the hiring process," Genova said. She found salvation—and lucre—in social media, where technology proved immensely useful in developing networks of professionals.

"These steps get us back working," Genova said. "Once we're back working, we can start migrating toward work that suits us and pays a king's ransom. How long does that take? To get back working, about three weeks. To get work that suits us and pays a king's ransom, about twenty-four to thirty-six months."

Genova knows that to start all over again, you have to accelerate your efforts; indeed, you need to be relentless.

I used to know a man who did exactly that. His name was Steven A. Martindale, and he was very good about managing change. He was a Washington lawyer and lobbyist famous for his access to socialites and for the parties he gave. But when he first came to Washington after his graduation from Stanford University on the staff of Senator Charles E. Goodell, Republican of New York, Martindale was a genuine nobody. He was even more of a nobody when Goodell left the Senate in 1991.

But Martindale deeply resented being a nobody. A native of Pocatello, Idaho, he wanted status. He yearned for recognition. He knew that he had to start all over again.

To do that, he rented a house and sent out 2,000 invitations to a party. Those invitations went to everybody:

George Schultz, Henry Kissinger, the president, everybody. Nobody showed up. Martindale was sitting there eating hot dogs alone on a Saturday night because nobody came to his party. He did it again a week later. A few people came. He did it again a week after that, and more people came. Finally, I think Kissinger showed up at a party. All of a sudden Steve Martindale became the person you had to go to in order to see people in Washington. He had the drive and the steam to get that done, and he became very successful at it. (Martindale died in 1990 at the age of forty-six of complications from AIDS.)

Martindale possessed relentlessness and an ability to be totally focused on his goals. He knew how to prepare for starting all over again.

It can be done.

3

Think Innovation—Forget about Just Keeping Up

Power players stay alert to technical developments so that they can make smart judgment calls about what's a must-learn.

THIS IS A sad story. I won't use the name of the corporate executive because you probably know him.

This man was doing very well in 1989. My guess is that his compensation was around $250,000 a year. He lived with his family in Winnetka, Illinois, and was on the fast track in his company.

He refused to learn about technology in even the simplest terms. He assumed that others would do it for him. He never checked into databases and never went online to learn.

Before he knew it, he was hit by a tech tsunami. People in his company wondered why he didn't keep up with things, why he didn't respond, why it took him so long to react.

This man was given every opportunity by his peers and his boss. Today he is on the street. His work environment could not tolerate his indifference. Today he is sending out résumés, and no one is responding.

Everything is running at warp speed. You need to get out there and get ahead in your thinking. You need to push the envelope. That means going out and actively looking to see what technologies are out there, which ones are in the development stage, and how they all relate to your profession. Perhaps new software can help streamline your company's billings and accounts. Perhaps a new digital storage system could bring down the use of paper.

If you say to yourself, "Well, I'm just going to monitor what's going on and try to keep up," you will fall behind. That's not a good thing.

What you have to do is be a part of the invention of the future. You must be able to figure out what is going to happen and apply that foresight to your life, your business, and your social situation. Then you must raise the bar. Get people to follow up. You need to set new objectives. You need to take prudent risks. You have to go beyond where things are and what is obvious in the marketplace.

I learned many years ago that one key to success in business is to find things nobody else has come up with. In 1972, my team and I created the "Public Relations Audit," a special method of assessing the impact of a company's image and its public relations efforts. It was hugely effective and got us a tremendous amount of business. Now everybody is using the Public Relations Audit. In fact, it is outdated because the business has evolved, but in 1972 nobody had thought of it.

My colleagues and I had half dozen ideas like that every year. We lived on creative tension.

One could say with certainty that Wendy Kopp also lives with creative tension. She's famous now as the founder of Teach for America (TFA), a nonprofit organization that dispatches Ivy League graduates to teach for two years at some of the nation's toughest schools. But back in 1989, when she was still a student at Princeton University, Kopp very nearly was derailed by a professor's comments when she told him about her plan to start a "Peace Corps" consisting of Ivy Leaguers such as herself. Those young men and women would be embedded in some of the country's toughest schools and also would promote education in surrounding communities.

As he recounted the episode later, the professor, Marvin Bressler, said to Kopp: "My dear Ms. Kopp, you are quite evidently deranged."

But Kopp wasn't one to be fazed. She went ahead and started Teach for America. She turned to the corporate sector for sponsorship and was able to rope in Union Carbide and Mobil, among others. She confounded skeptics, including some in academia and the media. When an error-filled article by an academician led some donors to withdraw, Kopp responded by publicly correcting each error. She also trimmed her budget and cut her staff. Today, so great is the demand from Ivy League applicants for positions at TFA that Kopp accepts only one out of every eight. The CEO of the United Negro College Fund, Michael Lomax, told *U.S. News & World Report* that Kopp's organization is one of the best-managed nonprofits he's ever seen.

The idea that Kopp implemented was that you have to stay ahead of the curve. She recognized that there was a pressing need to supplement the teaching staff at public schools, especially in low-income areas. By inducting Ivy League graduates into her organization, Kopp was being innovative: She was providing opportunities for those young men and women to "do good" soon after emerging from the cocoon of academia; at the same time she was addressing a genuine community need for dedicated teachers. Kopp developed her own technology network so that "her" teachers could stay connected no matter where their assignments were. She created her own model for business. Kopp's ideas came from keen observation, and they developed velocity from her belief that every student in the United States is entitled to a good school education.

The lesson is that you cannot let yourself just be current or be satisfied with the status quo. You cannot pick up *The Wall Street Journal* one day, go to Walter Mossberg's popular technology column, and say, "Mossberg has written about some new gadget that would be very useful in my daily business life. I should get that." You should have known about that gadget well before Mossberg reviewed it. How? Cultivating sources in the technology business is a good way to start. Nowadays, few offices can dispense with technology and its many manifestations. Gadgets are meant to improve productivity. That means that every business should have its sensors placed in the technology industry.

Remember, however, that gadgets are just that: gadgets. You can be armed with the most sophisticated hardware in the world and still bomb.

It is what you do with the gadgets, the intellectual property you drive, that will make a difference. Wendy Kopp's ideas fueled her Teach for America venture, and technology was simply something that helped her enhance her organization's work.

Another example that's worth citing is that of Solomon Trujillo, an American of Mexican heritage. When he became CEO of Australia's largest telecommunications company, Telstra, one of the first things he did was to ensure that the company's videoconferencing system was upgraded. By installing a video system worldwide, Trujillo gave himself instant access to his far-flung executives, enabling him to be updated continually about technological and economic developments in different parts of the world.

Trujillo knows, of course, that it takes more than the installation of the latest technology to become a successful power player. Besides the canny use of technology, his methodology for success centers on three pillars.

"To win, you must understand the needs of the customer," Trujillo told me. "You need to have a competitive cost structure. And you must have the right platforms. Ultimately, as a CEO, you need to ask yourself: How does creating a company based on a competitive model work toward providing for the social good of an entire country?"

That's a question I pose in various surveys. In our firm, we conduct more than a thousand interviews each year with people around the world. We interview them on social conditions, economic conditions, all kinds of different trends that shape the world. In the course of those thousand interviews we come up with things that are going to happen and that are going to be different in technology. Thus, if we use the information properly, we know way in advance what's going to happen. That's a significant undertaking for our company, and we take it very seriously.

For example, one of the companies we work with is called SearchHelp. It has created a device that eliminates pornography from children's computers. This is a huge breakthrough. Parents like it; libertarians don't. It's something to be reckoned with. We are ahead of the pack by knowing what it's all about, and that's an important thing.

By the time this book is published, preparations will be well under way for the 2008 presidential election in the United States. For everyone in business and in the professional world, this is going to be an important election. Therefore, it will be essential to think about the different policies and programs being proposed, not just domestically but internationally. As a power player, you should be thinking geopolitically regardless of your personal politics because the 2008 election, perhaps more than other recent elections, is going to shape the country's currently battered standing in the world community.

Technology is going to be a critical part of global geopolitics. What happens in China and India is going to be very important for the American economy, and it's useful to understand that. Why? Because China, along with several east Asian countries with bulging foreign exchange reserves, is buying up U.S. securities and Treasury bonds. This inflow of cash helps the United States deal with its trade imbalance and budget deficit. What if the Chinese decide to park their cash in euros instead? What if the next American president is a protectionist who opposes the exportation of jobs to third world countries where labor and production costs are significantly lower than they are in the United States? I'm not saying that bad things are going to happen, but I'm urging power players to be tuned in to global affairs. What happens out there affects us in here.

It also will be useful to study what Bill Gates, Steve Ballmer, Larry Ellison, and others in Silicon Valley say is going to happen so that you can position yourself for the future. Read *The Economist*. Read the reports prepared by the Economist Intelligence Unit, Ian Bremmer's Eurasia Group, and Strategic Foresight, Inc. (StratFor). Subscribe to trade publications in your field and beyond.

The best executives I have known over the years always look beyond the horizon. One approach I recommend was demonstrated by Robert Weissman, who used to run Dun & Bradstreet. He actually broke up the company into four different parts. Weissman was technologically brilliant. He sat at his computer virtually every working minute of the day: answering e-mails, looking things up on Google, checking the Edgar file, tapping into chat rooms and databases. Perhaps more than any other executive I've come across, he had mastered the technology that was driving the business and life at that time.

Bob Weissman figured out how to start new companies and how to make money and how to add value. He is smart. However, he did not do it alone. He used technology to gather the key information he needed.

I'm convinced that even with the breakup of Dun & Bradstreet and Weissman's retirement, Bob Weissman is sitting there today, Googling, going into eBay, checking out Lexis-Nexis, and much more, on a 24/7 basis.

I know another CEO who runs a Fortune 10 company. He has numerous people who work constantly on elements of technology. The challenge for those people is to come to him with a precise summary of what they are trying to say. If they came in with reams of paper or clutches of printouts, this guy would shove them out the door. What they've got to come in with is one, two, or three sentences that distill what he wants to know about.

What does he want to know about? He wants to know about trends that affect the sale of his products in different parts of the world. He wants to know about social attitudes that are going to change the sales of his products one way or another in different parts of the world. He wants to know what his competitors are doing. He wants to know about employee morale in his company. He wants to know on a minute-by-minute basis what the stock market is thinking, about his securities, and how he should adjust in relation to what is being said. All those factors come into play. He could sit there behind the computer and try to get it all himself, but it would be impossible to do that in the time he has available. Therefore, he has farmed this work out to seven or eight people in his organization, and they come to him virtually every hour and give him reports on what's happening. I call this anticipatory management. The lesson here is that CEOs must have their staff on the same page they are on. The CEO's suite should be a finely tuned machine that responds to the leader's directives.

I know another executive who runs a huge asset management company. He sits behind his desk reading reports, reading the newspaper, occasionally reading *Playboy*. Every ten or fifteen minutes one of his many traders bursts into the room and gives him a report on something that is happening in the market. He always says something incisive to that trader like, "I need to see the exact thing; I need to get exactly this type of data; I need to get behind the news." The trader literally runs out of the room and gets it off the PC by Googling or going to the available databases and comes back and says to the asset manager, "Here's what it is." At that point the asset manager says, "Buy 5,000" or "Sell 5,000." I've been in this man's office when he has made $400 million in one trade like that in the course of one day.

Making that kind of money, of course, is something reserved only for geniuses or the very lucky. But you don't have to wait for lightning to strike to make your fortune. The big players have access to the same technology as the most junior traders. It's learning how to see patterns in money movements and then acting on your hunches that account for success.

The point is that regardless of whether you are a head honcho or a junior trader, you've got to develop your filter for information to a degree you've never done before. You can learn to develop this filter only by studying the "masters of the universe" in your business. Their success, after all, did not come overnight. Most Wall Street icons I know, such as John Gutfreund and Felix Rohatyn, are always willing to share their experience and know-how. No matter how good the technology is, you are circumscribed by the fact that you are awake only seventeen or eighteen hours a day. In that period of time you can ingest and process only so much information. You have to say to yourself, "Where can I get this information?" or, "How fast can I get it, and how quickly can I ingest it? How quickly can I turn it on and do something with it?" You have to be alert to the changes that are taking place daily in cyberspace. Having a mentor or guide definitely helps.

You have to be able to identify the right sources of information in this digital age. There is so much gibberish out there and there are so many untruths. You need to learn how to anticipate actively what's happening in the technology field. This requires more than surfing the Web or reading technical magazines. You need to cultivate people in the industry, get them to trust you, and sustain your relationships in a mutually beneficial manner.

However, the most important thing, at least to me, is that you acquire information with integrity and ethics and a sense of dignity and properness. One executive said to me, "Look on the Internet—you can just type anything in, make all kinds of grammatical errors. Punctuation doesn't have to be there; you can use the letter *u* for *you*." I often say to myself, I guess that's right, but I don't think much about it because we are diminishing a hierarchy of standards that we've had for ages. Shorthand is simply not elegant, and in my view it's disrespectful to the recipient. I realize that I'm voicing a minority view here, but so be it. Language and nuance are very important, and even in e-mails they should not be treated cavalierly.

I understand that it is difficult for most people to identify the technology that is on the horizon. They can't do it because they lack the technical literacy or simply lack the vision to see beyond their present predicament. Not everyone can afford expensive trade publications. Not everyone is in a position to phone Bill Gates and ask what's on his mind. But you'd be surprised how much useful information you can glean from magazines and newspapers and Web sites. You need to set aside a specific time each day to read. My 40-minute commute to Manhattan from my Connecticut home constitutes not just a journey but a period of intensive reading. Ideas come to me, and I jot them down on my PDA.

To look beyond the horizon, I also encourage you to read unconventional publications regardless of your political persuasion. You must read *Mother Jones*, the *Utne Reader*, and the *New York Review of Books*. Seek out veteran editors such as Robert Silvers and Lewis Lapham. You'd be surprised how accessible they can be if you approach them politely and sincerely. Invite them to lunch. Listen carefully. Don't ask them for literary favors; just take copious notes.

There are also people tucked away in universities and think tanks whom you should contact. You may think that I'm making a naive suggestion here, but most academicians I know are flattered when an outsider asks to attend their lectures. Paul Kennedy, the Yale historian, is one who comes to mind, as do New York University's Ralph Buultjens and John Brademas. Columbia's trade specialist Jagdish Bhagwati is another, as is South Asia specialist Arvind Panagariya. Richard N. Haass, president of the Council on Foreign Relations, is still another. They have insights that are extraordinary. Difficult though it might be to get time with any of them because they are busy people, if you can do that, you will find that it beats any blog or anything on the Internet.

David Dunlap is another person you might have wished to seek out. Dunlap was a paraplegic and he is gone now, but he was a wizard when it came to numerous issues in Pennsylvania. Dunlap needed help to get into the office, but he'd immediately get behind his desk and start working. He was responsible for almost of the energy regulation that took place in Pennsylvania. He knew the ins and outs, the commas and the paragraphs of what was going to take place. If you wanted to know about energy regulation, Dunlap was the go-to guy. There's also Edward Morse at Lehman Brothers on Wall Street, a walking encyclopedia on global energy issues.

There are people like these in every field, and if you try to find out who they are and tap into them, you will have a lot of fun. You will learn a lot, and your life will be better because of it. Moreover, if people know that you know those people and are able to understand them, they'll come to you because they don't know those people and have no way of getting to them.

Just what should you be asking in your conversation with Kennedy or Bhagwati or Morse or any other luminary who is willing to meet with you?

One simple, central question: "Why?"

You're trying to figure out why certain things happen or why they are taking place. I offer the example of William Berkley, the business and insurance genius, who's based in Greenwich, Connecticut. He is intellectually brilliant and is never satisfied with anything except the answer to the question "Why?" He wants to know that. He'll offer opinions; he will offer views; he'll come up with facts. But the answer to the question, "Why is this taking place?" is extremely important to him. He's humble enough to ask that question of just about anyone he meets, and people are flattered that he would ask them that question.

For a successful entrepreneur like Berkley, it is important to gain understanding of all the different points of view relating to his business. He also recognizes that no single one of them is the ultimate point of view. That is the first step. Then you must understand how the kernel that you come to leads to a solution to a problem.

Here's an example of what I mean: There is a company that had a big operation in the Bahamas, and it tried to build a hotel. It couldn't build the hotel because of union problems, delivery of things, and so on. It asked me to try to figure out what was happening, and I did a lot of research.

Before I was to present my research at a public meeting, one of the people in the company, who was kind of a firebrand, said to me, "If these people won't let us build the hotel, here's what we are going to do to the island."

I said, "The island really doesn't care, John, but here is the problem you have. The Mafia is holding all this up, and if you don't figure a way to deal with the Mafia other than through illegal payments, you are never going to get the hotel built, or, if you get it built, it will be a faulty construction."

I had sought advice from forty people before I offered my counsel, but my client rejected my advice.

"It's not the Mafia," one executive said.

I said, "Fine, if it's not the Mafia, there must be another reason why you're having problems getting your hotel built. So go ahead and build the hotel, pour the concrete. There might be a body or two in it where you pour it, and your hotel won't be satisfactory once you finish it. You've got to figure out a way to deal with the Mafia."

The executive said, "What's the way to deal with the Mafia?"

I said, "You should go to the FBI. Get the FBI to talk to the government of the island and get rid of these guys; that's what you need to do. Try to find a direct linkage to somebody in the FBI through a local field office and then go to the head of the FBI and get this done."

My clients did just that, and they got the hotel built.

The point is that if I had not done all that research, if I had not coalesced all those points of view into a single recommendation, they probably still would be sitting there, ten years later, not having built the hotel, complaining, being at odds with the island and the leadership in the island, and not reaping the economic advantages that eventually came their way. The lesson here is that it wasn't enough just to "keep up" with developments; I needed to look beyond the horizon, figure things out, and draft my advice accordingly.

Being a power player is a full-time effort. You need to be thinking out your strategies continuously; you need to figure out how to tap into new sources of information. You need to make quick decisions about what's relevant to your business and what's not. If you want to be a serious power player, you must be reconciled to the fact that you're in it for the long haul. Microsoft wasn't built in a day, and neither was Apple.

4

Seize the Opportunity in Every Crisis

Technology enhances your professional prospects regardless of your setbacks and may even help you become an independent entrepreneur.

THERE'S ALWAYS SOME crisis or other going on in the world and in our personal lives. The question is, How do we deal with that crisis?

That question has become more acute because we've never been in a time when the world, the country, business sectors, families, and social institutions have been under fire more than they are today. We are in one of the most uncertain times in history. The ability to survive in an uncertain time is critical.

Things are going to happen out there that we do not expect. Many political and business leaders, among others, assert that one of the great challenges is the rift between the Muslim world and the West. I disagree with that assessment. That is certainly a great challenge, but the bigger challenge is the growing chasm between the haves and the have-nots. The World Bank estimates that nearly 2 billion of the world's 6 billion-plus people live on the equivalent of less than a dollar a day. Meanwhile, Wall Street is paying out annual bonuses of $40 or $50 million to some CEOs. A trader I know took home $100 million in 2006. We are going to have to find meaningful ways to eliminate global poverty in our lifetime, and that means finding an opportunity in a crisis.

The singer Bono found just such an opportunity. As the lead singer of the rock band U2, Bono has all the money and adulation in the world. He decided that global poverty is too overwhelming to take on all at once, and so he began to focus on Africa, the poorest continent. He persuaded Paul O'Neill, the Alcoa CEO who was then President George W. Bush's treasury secretary, to accompany him to Africa.

That trip generated a lot of publicity, as Bono knew it would. He knew that there was an opportunity to get positive action by drawing attention to Africa's humanitarian crisis. Sure enough, the wealthy nations of the world soon pledged to increase investment, developmental aid, and technical assistance. Africa's problems, of course, are so enormous that it will take many decades for the people of that continent to attain prosperity, but instead of joining the global chorus of despair, Bono spotted an opportunity for engendering change in Africa and acted on it. He made videos that could be downloaded easily on personal computers; he cut records; he made podcasts. Bono employed all the tools that modern technology offers to a determined celebrity with a cause.

This sort of action takes perspicacity. However, most people tend to wallow in misery when confronted by a personal crisis. A man I know found himself out of his high-profile CEO job. Automatically, he wasn't part of "the club" any longer. Invitations to A-list parties suddenly dried up. He began to develop palpitations. His blood pressure shot up. I encouraged him to let go. His company's decision to let him go was irreversible, and so I told him to pause and cleanse his mind of the trauma, difficult though that would be. I encouraged him to do deep breathing exercises. "Find a way to control your metabolism, your body, so that you are able to adapt and adjust to this turbulent time and be able to deal with it," I said.

This man joined a yoga class. One evening, as he was preparing for a lesson, it occurred to him that there might be a business opportunity there. Yoga had not taken off yet in the United States. He launched an enterprise that included yoga franchises. He saw an opportunity in his personal crisis.

I know how humiliating it is to go through a professional crisis. I also know how important it is to have the support of friends during such a time. Within two days of my leaving Hill & Knowlton, I was called by a woman named Myrna Blyth. She was the editor of *Ladies' Home Journal* and a great friend.

"I'm taking you to lunch," Myrna said.

Knowing that Myrna would suggest the Four Seasons, I said, "But Myrna, I don't think that I would be able to pay for the lunch."

"I'm paying," Myrna said. "And we are going to the Four Seasons."

Myrna's status and stature were such that they always gave her a prominent table in the restaurant's Grill Room, the power lunch place. I was nervous, not knowing what to expect. Myrna was very generous and decent.

"We are going to sit here for two hours, and people are going to see us together," she said.

That was all we did, and it was very effective. People would come over and say nice things to Myrna, and Myrna would talk about the fact that I was starting a new business and she hoped that the person who stopped at our table would give me support. We just sat there, and we had a wonderful time, but it had nothing to do with the lunch. There was a perception of being seen, and every power broker in the restaurant that day came by and said something. That changed the entire paradigm. Myrna Blyth, without saying so specifically, saw an opportunity for me and acted on her instinct. I'll never forget that.

Myrna was exercising power, however subtly. I once asked my friend Allan E. Goodman, president and CEO of the Institute of International Education—a big power player, not least because he also runs the Fulbright scholars program—about how he viewed power players and their ability to respond to crises.

This is what Dr. Goodman told me: "They are not impressed with power, and they are not concerned with power. They are concerned with ideas and impact. To me, that's the biggest lesson I've learned from the people I've met. Their focus, and the focus of any of us that are lucky enough to lead an institution, has got to be what you do with it. How you make the world less dangerous, how you make your community a better place, how you energize people to get their ideas, because you don't have all the ideas yourself. The best leaders focus on getting the best ideas and then doing something with them."

A person I admire precisely because he always acts on opportunities is Professor Sreenath Sreenivasan. As of this writing, he's dean of students at Columbia University's

Graduate School of Journalism. He's barely thirty-six years old. He helped create the New Media program at Columbia in 1994, and now he's the nation's indisputable authority on the uses of the Internet. When asked about how he came upon that opportunity, Sreenivasan said: "When I discovered new media and the Internet, it was to me a moment like seeing color television for the first time. I remember that excitement. I remember the moment I first saw a Web site. And those days it was very dull and just a bunch of text, but the opportunity there of having, literally, the whole world open up to you was very promising. And I saw this as something that was going to change our lives. It's going to change my life for sure, especially as someone who is interested in telling stories about our world and its issues.

"What I have seen, and why I continue to teach new media, is that there is just so much that is unknown about this—we're evolving the standards of new media. I compare it very often to working in radio at the turn of the last century or working in television in the early 1950s, when nobody knew what would happen. There are no rules; we're just trying to decide what will happen. We're trying to handle the technology in a way where it's effective and does what it's supposed to. There is just too much confusion out there. There is too much frustration that everyday people have because computers don't work necessarily the way they're supposed to. You can imagine a young person, or an old person, who goes online for the first time, anywhere in the world—how much more exciting and, at the same time, how much more scary it is at this point in time. Especially internationally, to go online and see both the wonderful opportunities and the challenges when you first come across a Web site."

When I asked Sreenivasan about how he spots opportunities in any technological crisis, this is how he responded:

"With any new technology, any new medium, there is a sense of people not being sure where it's going to lead. People are entrenched in an old medium or have stakes in the old medium—unless they are open, unless their minds are open, they are very likely to fight it. And we saw that, in fact, with new media here, with the evolution of the World Wide Web. People in radio and television and print in many ways fought it. Of course, other organizations went out of their way to embrace it. The biggest challenge really is for people to see that this particular medium won't just cannibalize the old media but will help improve them. It will help bring new audiences. It will tell stories and give information in ways that were never possible before."

Professor Sreenivasan is among the extraordinary men I've been privileged to meet during my career who were keenly observant, sensed change coming, and adapted to the culture.

There are many extraordinary people I never got a chance to meet because they lived in a different era. G. K. Chesterton was one. He demonstrated how powerful words are. Mohandas Karamchand Gandhi, the Mahatma, was another. He was a practitioner of power who wielded it subtly. He was truly a founder of independent India. There are figures like this, and they know how to handle themselves, what to say, and when to say it. Gandhi showed that stubbornness is a form of power. Stick to your principles and be as stubborn as you have to be if it's right. That's extremely important.

There are a lot of people who give up at the last moment or give in. If you believe in your principles, negotiating downward is crazy. If Gandhi believed that he was correct in his principles, why should he compromise?—and he didn't. Gandhi knew that there was a crisis in colonial India, that the British rulers were not about to give up what the novelist Paul Scott called the Jewel in the Crown of the empire.

Gandhi's story, although it ended tragically with his assassination by a fellow Hindu in January 1948, just a few months after the British granted independence to India, is especially relevant to our times. As far as I can tell, he was the first world leader to employ the technology of his time in the public interest. That technology flowed from the telegraph and found expression in radio and the microphone, which hugely enhanced Gandhi's ability to address tens of thousands of people at rallies.

In Gandhi's day there was no television. The main media consisted of newspapers, wire services, and radio. If Gandhi's fame spread, that was not because of the domestic media in India, all of which were controlled by the British or at least heavily censored, but because of foreign correspondents such as Robert Trumbull of *The New York Times*, James W. Michaels of United Press (later to become the editor of *Forbes*), Vincent Sheehan, and of course the photographer Margaret Bourke-White, whose picture of Gandhi at his spinning wheel is a classic. (In Sir Richard Attenborough's Oscar-winning film *Gandhi*, a character based on Bourke-White is played by Candice Bergen; Trumbull, Michaels, and Sheehan were melded into the character of an unnamed journalist played by Martin Sheen.)

Did Gandhi "manipulate" those foreign correspondents? Of course. Let's not forget that he was no stranger to the West. He had obtained his law degree in Britain, had practiced law in apartheid South Africa, and had traveled in Europe. Gandhi understood the power of the press. He also knew how the masses and the colonialists alike could be influenced by staged events such as the famous Salt March. Gandhi was well aware that the march, which he had undertaken to protest taxes imposed on salt production, would be filmed, photographed, and written about extensively by the foreign media.

Why do you think Gandhi traveled in third class in India's trains? It was the symbolism. He wanted to be portrayed as a man of the masses. Of course, when Gandhi occupied a third-class compartment, no passengers were allowed in other than his aides.

My point is that Gandhi was a skilled strategist as well as a tactician. He understood the pressure points to which the British colonialists would respond: pictures and reports in the foreign press. Gandhi was his own PR man; there were no public relations agencies in those days. He instinctively understood how the technology of that day could be put to use in the service of his cause: India's independence from the British.

I don't mean to sound cynical about Gandhi: He did what he had to do. But he was less a saint than a tough politician who knew exactly what the independence game was all about: mobilizing public opinion against the British not only in his native India, the Jewel in the Crown, but, perhaps even more important, overseas. In his homespun dhoti, Gandhi cut a frail figure. We now know, of course, that even that frailty was a carefully cultivated and robustly sustained image.

The Mahatma had an invaluable ally in his protégé, Jawaharlal Nehru, the Cambridge-educated scion of a wealthy aristocratic family who was to become independent India's first prime minister. Like Gandhi, Nehru understood the West. They complemented each other: Gandhi, the seemingly homespun skin-and-bones figure speaking out against the mighty British and speaking up for the preservation of India's cultural values, and Nehru, the dapper Kashmiri (and lover of Lady Mountbatten, wife of the viceroy, Lord Mountbatten, who was gay) who was what might be termed today telegenic.

In this carefully plotted scenario Gandhi represented the face of traditional India, and Nehru, the face of modernization for India but without the intrusive colonialism of the British.

They were both great communicators, and the media of that time lapped it all up. It was, of course, wonderful political theater, and Gandhi knew it, Nehru knew it, and Lord Mountbatten knew it (his was the voice that ultimately persuaded British Prime Minister Clement Atlee's government that it was best to leave India). The technology of the day enhanced their ability to reach the masses in a way that would have been unimaginable in the nineteenth century, when the Indian National Congress was founded by an English civil servant, Allan Octavian Hume.

All this isn't to say that it was a smooth ride for Gandhi and Nehru. After all, both did jail time; together they aggregated thirty years in prison. But those incarcerations played to a full house, as it were. The foreign media reported every detail. Prison was where Nehru wrote several of his books, including what I think was his greatest, *The Discovery of India*, which offers rich insights into Indian history.

Theirs was a great team: Messrs Gandhi & Nehru, Inc. In contemporary times they would have been awarded the Nobel Peace Prize and received multi-million-dollar book contracts, and their success would have spawned a prime-time TV series. But as history would have it, they had to settle for the independence of Britain's biggest, most populous, and most resource-rich colony.

It is, of course, an irony that the independent India they created would build on the technology that the duo used. In time, India would be an incubator for software companies and a source of computer programmers for Western companies. Perhaps it's even more ironic that the colonial British one day would outsource thousands of back-office jobs to Indians in India. Even Britain's flagship airline, British Airways, processes all its worldwide ticket operations in India.

It is also ironic that Nehru's grandson, Rajiv Gandhi, introduced computers to India's government in the 1980s, when he became prime minister after the assassination of his mother and Nehru's only daughter, Prime Minister Indira Gandhi. It was Rajiv who spurred investment in technology research and encouraged the private sector to explore the technology sector, which was still in its infancy. Today India exports billions of dollars each year in hardware, software, and technology services.

Gandhi and Nehru had the force of personality that didn't need embellishment or enhancement by what today's PR types offer. Their integrity and their own words were persuasive. No sound bites or cue cards were necessary for them, although their speeches and writings still are widely read for the insights they offer into India's history.

Let's also not forget that the Gandhi-Nehru "communications success" indeed had PR help from India's population of 200 million (there are more than a billion Indians now). Those everyday Indians provided the word-of-mouth support and what today's communications maestros might call *buzz* that no formal national PR campaign could create.

There was also what today's marketing gurus would call *felt demand*. Indians were fed up with British colonial rule; the imperialists had been in India for 150 years. Thus the Gandhi-Nehru message resonated well among the masses: Indians yearned for independence, and the Gandhi-Nehru team echoed their aspirations and gave voice to the popular ethos in a way that made international audiences, including the audience in Britain, respond favorably.

The team cast the struggle for independence in simple moral terms: It was wrong for the British to stay, it was right for them to leave; it was wrong for Indians to be subjected to the yoke of continued colonial rule, it was right that they obtain self-governance. In effect, Gandhi and Nehru said that India needed new rules of governance, and the first new rule called for self-rule.

In short, Gandhi and Nehru seized the high moral ground. There was nothing that the British could offer as a credible response.

My own view, perhaps a revisionist one, is that although chronologically it took several decades for Gandhi and Nehru to drive out the British, the battle for independence was won the day they joined hands. It was a power partnership.

That partnership was engendered by mutual admiration and mutual need: Gandhi, the home-bred nationalist, and Nehru, the foreign-educated convert to the cause. India surely would have gained independence without their teamwork, but it would have taken much longer.

Their partnership also was anchored in respect and affection for the British people. Gandhi and Nehru never resorted to the rhetoric of violence and venality that characterized so many of colonial Africa's independence movements. Indeed, Gandhi espoused the doctrine of *ahimsa*—nonviolence—and Nehru was an abashed admirer of Bertrand Russell, John Russell, Henry David Thoreau, and Ralph Waldo Emerson, all of whom wrote extensively about how peace must be paramount and how the end do not justify the means.

That respect and affection for Britons eventually resulted in the strongest political, economic, and cultural relationship between a colonial power and an ex-colony, and that relationship survives to this day. The Queen's English is still spoken in India—with accommodations for local idioms, of course—and Indian institutions of governance still are modeled after their British counterparts. Indian students may travel in increasing numbers to the United States, but they have not abandoned Oxbridge (Oxford and Cambridge). Savile Row tailoring still is coveted among the Indian elite, and of course there's a maniacal obsession with a British export, cricket.

Could Gandhi and Nehru have foreseen all this? That's one of the imponderables of history. However, the fact that there is a healthy living British legacy in the daily life of India suggests a validation of an important belief of Gandhi and Nehru: The most worthwhile political victories are the ones in which the victors and the vanquished end their battle in amity and mutual respect, and it is important to look for opportunities in any crisis, however seemingly intractable.

I was scarcely born when Gandhi and Nehru led India to independence, but I often hark back to their experience in my study of the power game. The duo fulfilled the ultimate objective of any power game: to make change happen. How many of us get the opportunity to liberate an entire subcontinent?

I would have loved to have been there during India's struggle for independence. What a laboratory for the power game! Some of my work these days involves advising companies on doing business with India, and I'm continually amazed by the economic emergence of this nation; Gandhi and Nehru couldn't possibly have imagined the India of 2007, an international powerhouse whose economic might is eclipsing that of its former ruler, Great Britain.

As my own career developed, I did get a chance to observe other power players display their skills. One situation that I was personally involved with took place in Indianapolis. I was approached by a man named Zane Todd, who ran a business called the Indianapolis Power & Light Company. It was important to the power company to develop jobs and expedite economic growth in the city. I was asked to develop a plan.

That plan ranged from bringing in the prestigious think tank the Hudson Institute to getting the Baltimore Colts to move to Indianapolis. All that happened, and the center of the city was rejuvenated.

But I'm getting ahead of the story. Before the plan could be implemented, some sticky problems had to be dealt with. The most significant one was the fact that Indianapolis had an active chapter of the racist Ku Klux Klan. There were race-related employment issues too. At that time, there was an old-boy network that was not open and did not embrace new people in Indianapolis, and that was clearly a problem. There was exclusivity in Indianapolis.

When I prepared the plan and went to Todd, he said: "I can't possibly take this before the city fathers."

I said, "Why not?"

He said, "It will make them all extremely angry, and they'll toss you out, they'll toss me out; we won't make any progress."

We were in a crisis. I had to think fast about a solution.

"Why don't we go to Gene Pulliam?" I said. Pulliam ran the Pulliam newspapers, which included the *Indianapolis Star* and the *Arizona Republican Gazette*. He was probably the most powerful man in the city and a real Hoosier.

Zane Todd did exactly that. He previewed the plan for Pulliam, and Pulliam said: "My God, we have to get rid of the Klan; we have to break down these barriers; we've got to do all the things the plan says."

Whereupon Todd said, "Gee, I don't think we can possibly do that. No one here is going to want to accept this. First of all, they don't want to acknowledge the fact that we have these problems. And second, they probably don't want to solve them."

"Well, let's have a meeting with all these people," Pulliam said.

The meeting was held at the Columbia Club, one of the swankiest clubs in Indianapolis. There were probably forty of the top people in Indianapolis there. First of all, as Todd had predicted, they were unwilling to admit that the Ku Klux Klan was there; they were unwilling to admit that there was exclusivity; they were unwilling to admit that racism existed in the city. Also, they were unwilling to acknowledge that we had made a very persuasive case, even using graphics to illustrate the major changes we had proposed for the city.

The meeting quickly turned sour. There was name-calling; there was unseemly abuse. It wasn't pretty.

Pulliam had kept quiet during the entire hullabaloo. Then he suddenly stood up and walked over to the door. He put his hand on the doorknob. Because of who Pulliam was, a quiet came over the room.

"I'm going to have to leave the room now, and I'm not going to come back because it's clear you don't want to deal with reality," Pulliam said in a matter-of-fact tone. "Unless you are willing to accept this plan, I'm leaving the room now."

He started to open the door. Then one man came running across the room and said, "Mr. Pulliam, please don't leave."

The gathering of august citizens in Indianapolis then quickly embraced the plan to rejuvenate their city.

What was actually taking place was that the real power player—Gene Pulliam—never emerged from the shadows until the last minute. If you had set up a meeting like this properly in advance and knew what you were doing and had worked with the power player before the meeting actually took place, you could be relatively assured that success would be yours. The power player generally would sit very quietly like a mandarin in the meeting. At the right time the power player would stand up and do what Pulliam did.

Pulliam, of course, was playing the power game. He was able to project outwardly and see what life could be like under our plan. He perceived a crisis at that meeting, yet he also saw an opportunity. He waited for that one instant in time. Thus a big part of power lies in knowing the moment to move. It's not being all over the place all the time; it's knowing that one critical instant to move, taking action, and getting the result.

Whether or not the power players have the exact paradigm of what the future is going to be, they have a sense of it, and they know how to get there. They also know what steps along the way will have to be taken to get there, and they take those steps.

In the preface to his 1991 book *Managing for the Future: The 1990s and Beyond*, management guru Peter Drucker wrote, "The executive's world has been turbulent for as long as I can remember—I started work two years before the 1929 crash! It surely has always been turbulent, but never as much as in these past few years—or in the years immediately ahead. . . . There are enormous opportunities, because change is opportunity. But there is no predictability. Turbulence—for those who still remember a little mathematics—is characterized by having no predictability. It is certain that the unexpected will happen; but it is impossible to predict where, when, or how. We live in a very turbulent time, not because there is so much change, but because it moves in so many different directions. In this situation, the effective executive has to be able to recognize and run with opportunity, to learn, and constantly to refresh the knowledge base."

It was not for nothing that they called him a guru. Peter Drucker has passed away, but you would do well to heed his words.

5

Look beyond the New Rules to Connect

The growing demand is for whatever or whoever can capture attention. But one fundamental "rule" of the power game never becomes outdated: the importance of treating people with respect and courtesy. Always connect.

THE "RULES" OF power and influence are changing so fast that it's difficult to grasp. One needs to obtain a perspective—an early warning, as it were—of what's beyond the horizon.

It's December 26, a day when many in the world are starting to stir from the Christmas holiday. I open my e-mail and find that I've received links to seventeen blogs.

These are blogs about court cases, the 2008 presidential election, food, travel, personal diaries. I express surprise to my family: We are starting to enjoy a long holiday at La Semmana on St. Maarten. They all urge me to turn the blogs off and delete them, but I quickly skim each one.

I have a three-word suggestion for power players: Read the blogs. Did I read all seventeen? No, but I looked at the content of each one, read two, and forwarded two others.

Did it help me? You bet. I received information that could come from no other source.

Was it time-consuming? Not really. I've trained myself to do it quickly. The December 26 experience took about three minutes.

What exactly is a blog? The word combines two other words: *Web* and *log*. Nowadays it's more than a noun; it's become a verb as well, as in "I blog," "she blogs," "we blog." In fact, given the millions of blogs around, it's probably fair to say, "We all blog." According to Wikipedia, the online encyclopedia to which anyone can contribute, a blog is a user-generated Web site in which entries are made in journal style. In the old days, before the World Wide Web came along, bloggers were known as diarists or memoirists. Now blogs provide commentary or news on food, politics, local events, and even prurient matters.

In this case, seventeen bloggers sought me out. Was I flattered? No, but I did share their blogs. If I had wanted to go to dozens of other blogs, it would have been easy.

A salient feature of blogs is that they are interactive: Anyone can post a comment. Blogs often have links to other blogs and to the favorite Web sites of the blogger. Blogs are part of what's come to be known as social media. Indeed, *Time* magazine's Person of the Year for 2006 was "You," an acknowledgment that individuals all over the world are making a monumental imprint on the way we perceive, report, and write the news. Big corporations sometimes see themselves as vulnerable to gossip about their products, services, and management spread by bloggers. Some companies are even encouraging their executives to blog in an effort to get the "human" side of a company across to consumers.

Take the example of Sun Microsystems. More than 3,000 employees, or 10 percent of the company's workforce, are blogging heavily with the blessing of their bosses. Those blogs draw nearly 2 million page views each month. The employees blog about their corporation. They blog about the weather. They blog about what people wore to the annual meeting of shareholders. At times there are hints of naughtiness in the blogs.

Who is Sun's blogger in chief? The CEO himself, Jonathan Schwartz. His blog (http://blogs.sun.com/ jonathan) is translated into ten languages.

"The notion of the corporation as an ivory tower has just gone," Schwartz told the *San Jose Mercury News* recently.

News organizations also are featuring blogs on their Web sites. Journalists representing American media at the highest level believe that blogging will have an increasingly serious impact on traditional journalism, especially print journalism, and eventually could go mainstream. Every day more bloggers take to the Internet highway, communicating information that ranges from important information to unauthenticated hearsay to drivel.

Since the majority of Americans are not readers, there is no way to know how many read blogs; perhaps only bloggers read blogs. However, there is no doubt that bloggers are revealing news and information that traditional media miss or purposely avoid.

There is a second issue: With so many blogs out there, which ones should you read? Who do you know that you should be reading? We all know we should read *The Wall Street Journal*. It is an established authority, and we can get it almost anywhere in the world via the Internet, if not the print edition itself. But why should we read the blog of John Q. Smith? And how do we even know about it?

In an article titled, "Blogs Revolution," that appeared in *The Journalist*, a magazine published by the Society of Professional Journalists, Steven Levy said: "Smack in the middle of the tech revolution is none other than traditional journalism, both in the way it's practiced and (even more ominously) in the way it's funded." Levy added: "So it's not surprising that every so often, I get the impression that as an, um, mainstream journalist, I'm covering my own funeral."

It's obvious that blogs, podcasts, and mass postings from camera phones can outperform mainstream media, according to Levy. "All of that is great—unless it drives out too much of what's essential in mainstream media: well-funded, painstakingly researched dispatches by experienced professionals," Levy points out. "Disturbingly, while outposts of traditional journalism are laying off reporters, closing bureaus, and cutting expense budgets, their parent companies are on an acquisition binge that embraces the amateurs. . . . *The New York Times* paid $410 million for About.com, which hires freelance 'experts' who offer guidance on subjects ranging from knitting to cat care."

Levy says that traditional journalism is being assaulted not only by sites like craigslist, offering for "free all the things that used to be known as paid classified ads," but also by companies like Google and Yahoo! that increasingly are "siphoning off advertising bucks with their auction-based, laser-targeted Internet ads." In 2006, online advertising fetched $17 billion, and those revenues are likely to increase.

If you seek power and influence in the twenty-first century, you need to know how to master this area. At some point your company is going to have a Web presence, not to mention buying advertising on the Internet.

Nevertheless, you'd be surprised at how many companies, particularly small businesses, hesitate to have even a modest Web presence. Microsoft's worldwide head of small business, Eddie Yandle, says that one in five companies are "non-adopters of IT." Older business owners are fearful of technology, and many say that computers confuse them. Young entrepreneurs are far more likely to incorporate information technology in their workplaces.

"Younger business owners have the advantage of growing up with IT—installing a business application holds less fear for a generation that submitted its college work by e-mail and turns to the Internet to find anything from a holiday to a date," says Stephen Pritchard of the *Financial Times*. "Younger business owners—at least in the developed world—have also benefited from the falling cost of IT hardware and related services, such as broadband Internet."

A recent survey by Lexis-Nexis revealed that 50 percent of Americans watch network television to get the news. Radio ranks second with 42 percent, followed by local newspapers with 37 percent. Today, just 6 percent of the population turns to user groups, blogs, and chat rooms.

You can expect that to change dramatically.

According to Lexis-Nexis, 52 percent of Americans' favorite programs are entertainment, hobbies, weather, and food and cooking. Even though they choose traditional media for those topics, emerging media are the second most frequently used sources.

The Lexis-Nexis survey found that 52 percent of consumers claim they probably will continue to trust and use traditional news sources, whereas over 35 percent said they will trust and use a combination of traditional and emerging media. Thirteen percent said they mostly will use emerging media for news they consider authentic. Yet online journalists said at a recent annual meeting of Associated Press managing editors that their industry's survival "depends on how well they can engage and excite the masses of readers on the Web."

Referring to the digital age, Jim Brady, the executive editor of WashingtonPost.com, warned editors that "it's not as frightening as what will happen to journalism if we don't embrace [the Web]." He said that newspapers today compete not only with other newspapers but with Google, CNN, and blogs.

The world of print journalism will never be the same, according to media experts. The next few years should determine the fate of the mainstream or traditional journalism that has served the public for so many years. It's also important to remember that technology never takes a holiday. The rules of power will continue to factor in the seismic changes occurring in all types of industries— the mass media included—as a result of technological advances. Nonetheless, power players must not overlook the most critical "power rule" of all: The human element cannot be ignored.

No one knows that better than my associate of more than two decades, Joan Avagliano. I cannot imagine my business surviving without her acuity and know-how. I realize that she no doubt will ask for a hefty raise when she sees these comments about her, but Joan is simply indispensable. I trust her judgment and value her opinions.

I asked her for her thoughts on how she keeps abreast of technological developments that affect the communications industry and how she looks "beyond the new rules."

"Blogging," "Check the Internet, "Google a company," "Check your voice mail," "Don't forget your Treo." Avagliano said she was never taught all those terms when she graduated from the Katharine Gibbs secretarial school and Saint Peter's College.

"I thought for sure that filing and stenography and fast typing were going to carry the day. But not anymore," she said. "Today I use the Internet on a regular basis to look up telephone numbers and do research on my desktop computer; today I use e-mail to reach the assistants of various chief executives to set up meetings; today I can organize a dinner for twenty anywhere in the world just by using technology. I can see the room on my computer, issue the e-vites, and get confirmations within minutes. Whatever happened to nice printed invitations?"

All this technology has complicated Avagliano's life in many ways. Few people will take a phone message these days. She can leave a voice mail, that is, if she can get anyone to pick up the phone in the first place. Few people will make an appointment if their computers are down; they book everything online.

But in an industry like public relations and strategic communications, Avagliano has learned that connecting with people is a key to success.

"And I have to say, this holds true in everything related to industry," she says.

Leaving a voice mail message isn't really connecting. Sending an e-mail isn't always the final answer. Several people have told her that they sent an e-mail that she never received, and no one called to follow up on it.

Joan Avagliano knows that by speaking with people, by communicating with them in writing, by sending a small gift to thank someone for extending himself or herself, you build relationships and networks that will last. You may know how to network, but it's how you keep the network alive that will be key to your progress.

It's a matter of breaking through all the technology and layers of people that will lead to success.

The other day Avagliano called the office of a CEO of a Fortune 50 pharmaceutical company to follow up on a letter she'd sent requesting a meeting. First, the operator for the company asked for her name, her company, and the reason for the call. No call would be put through to the CEO's office without that information. She finally reached the "executive office" receptionist, who told her that she would take a message and that the "chief of staff" would be returning her call. Ten minutes was wasted in all this. Avagliano never heard from the chief of staff. Her subsequent efforts to establish contact were similarly frustrating.

Is that how CEOs wish to be perceived? No longer can you call the CEO's office and actually get his or her assistant, who will take a message. Now they have to check the "log" for your letter, but the computer is down; now you have to talk to three assistants before you get to the one who handles the schedule.

There are exceptions, of course. One day Avagliano needed to reach the office of the president of one of the world's largest retail operations to determine whether he would receive a call about a potential business opportunity. The president actually answered his own phone. Avagliano asked him the question, and he urged her to have someone call him. Thus, in minutes she was able to make a connection that has worked out very well for the retailer.

One evening, a coworker at our office told Avagliano that he was in serious trouble because he couldn't reach his mortgage banker. He said that he was about to lose the deal on a house his wife really wanted. It was six o'clock in New York when he told her that; you could be sure no banker was on the job at that late hour on the East Coast. Fortunately, his bank was headquartered on the West Coast. Therefore, Avagliano suggested a call to the CEO's office in California. She spoke with his assistant and explained the problem. The assistant put Avagliano in touch with an executive vice president. The bank didn't want to lose out on the deal because it was a large mortgage. The end result? The closing took place earlier than expected.

Joan Avagliano has been my right-hand person for more than two decades. During that time she has come into contact with many interesting people, but few genuinely impress her intellectually. One who does is a man who works out of St. Louis and has counseled businesses and organizations on international relations for three decades. His name is Michael Fagin, and he knows how to use the new technical tools while still observing the basic rules of doing business.

When Avagliano asked Fagin about those rules, he said: "A baseline has got to be a person-to-person relationship. And that relationship has to be nurtured through direct communication—that is, speaking on the phone or seeing the person, even through a videoconference facility. Nothing will replace sitting down and working out arrangements of any business, civic, governmental, or philanthropic proposal."

To be sure, Fagin uses all the technological tools that are available to assist him in his work. For instance, each morning he scans dozens of publications on his computer to stay current with developments around the world. His research includes looking at English-language translations of articles written in scores of other languages. That would not be possible without the Internet.

However, the important thing, Fagin says, is "taking this information, and dissecting it, and passing all the valuable nuggets and their meaning to those who need to know—not just sending along the article for them to read. This takes brainpower, not manipulation of the keyboard."

Fagin seldom fails to emphasize that the tools are there for everyone and that each person uses different tools to reach his or her goals: e-mail, BlackBerry, Treo. Whatever these technological tools may be, they are just that: tools that help create the final product. They are the means, not the end.

He also emphasizes another point that I think is critical as we try to look beyond the new rules of the power game. "The complacency, and apathy, and learning curve still—and will always—reside in human-to-human contact, and without that in the forefront of learning there will always be a decrease in productivity going forward," Fagin says. "You can transmit a thought through e-mail— but you cannot [truly] transmit personal taste, cultural differences, and beliefs."

People who are accustomed to the use of technology in their lives often think that when they click the button, the job is done, the message has been conveyed, the response has been sent. However, there may be no follow-up, no direct contact to talk about what has been transmitted. This creates the "apathy and complacency" in decision making that Fagin talks about.

Avagliano adds: "And if you think that by clicking the button, the order has been placed and never call to follow up, never speak with someone who is handling the matter—and this person is out of the office—the order will never be done. Then, two weeks later, you find that you are two weeks behind schedule because you never followed up. At the very least, this results in a loss of productivity; I dare say it can also result in the loss of your job."

The point is that new rules or not, the human connection is irreplaceable. Apathy and complacency cannot take over and rule the day. We must remain responsible for our own actions; we cannot place all our trust in electronic media.

Fagin feels strongly, as do Avagliano and I, that follow-up is a key to success. "How many people follow up [personally] these days? Many people don't because they believe it is all done through electronic communication," he says.

How often do people rely on the spell-check on their word processors? All the time. But if you use the wrong word, it's not going to be caught. Apathy and complacency are setting in and breaking down productivity.

You can have the greatest PowerPoint presentation, but if the content is wrong or if the presentation is not what the client was expecting, you have just wasted a lot of time and money and probably will not get the business you are seeking.

Today people use the Internet even for online dating. Even though 12 percent of all marriages in 2006 reportedly involved people who met on the Internet, isn't it a bit difficult to transfer emotions over the Web?

"There is a simple equation we all should follow: We are individuals with a unique commodity, we bring value, we perform a task (using whatever means available), and we must follow up and make human contact and complete the task at hand," Avagliano says.

As she makes clear, each day is different, and there are always new devices and ways of getting to the end result. But ultimately it's all about knowing how to break through the clutter and not being stymied by the technology. Use it in the right way, but don't let it get in the way of your success.

Always look for a higher purpose. Every single person gets up in the morning and says, "How am I going to make enough money to pay the rent and take care of my food bill?" I understand that, but there needs to be a higher purpose in terms of what you do in your life. Society is tough enough. A lot of people have a pretty hard time out there.

The values of the old world still hold true: respect for other people, honoring your promises. On Wall Street there used to be a phrase, "Your word is your bond." Today, with the proliferation of lawyers, I think it's important that we still have a value like that.

If you look beyond the new rules, you will find the old ones, the enduring ones: It's the ability to be gracious, the ability to be decent. It's the ability to look for a higher purpose. It's the ability to give back. All those things are values that must be inherent in you or that you must adopt if you are going to be a power player.

And most of those values will never be made evident on the Web.

As I look at the CEOs of twenty years ago versus the CEOs of today, often the CEOs of today are tech CEOs. The CEOs of twenty years ago were the old industry CEOs; they were much more leaders of the community. The current tech CEOs are into themselves, into making money, and all wrapped up in their companies. What they ought to do is find a way to reach out to share some of that wealth, to draw people in, to make people part of the picture. That's what the old-time CEOs did, and it was one of the reasons the United States was as strong as it was: We had business, society, and politics all working together. Today we have business, society, and politics working in a very adversarial way.

People who are power players today could change that if they wanted to. They could make a major statement about the rules of the power game.

Whether you are in your neighborhood, your church, or your social club, you can use these values just as easily as the CEO of Exxon Mobil or Xerox can. They stand the test of time no matter what walk of life you are in. What's really important, however, is that if you use these values, they will help you get ahead. They will help you develop your career. They will help you improve your standard of living. They will put more money in your pocket. You do this not necessarily by taking advantage of people or taking advantage of a situation, but people on the outside will see that you are somebody with whom people can work.

If you are in a social group in Nebraska, belong to a church in Louisiana, or are a small business owner in Colorado or Ohio, these values will work for you. When they are applied properly, they can take you to a new level. At that new level you'll have experiences you never had before. Your life will be better. Your range of contacts will be better. You'll make more money. You'll have opportunities that never presented themselves before. It's all a matter of figuring out how to apply these values to your daily life.

What you need to do is connect those enduring values to the rules of the professional game. Then you are likely to become a sterling power player.

6

Take the Heat
and Never Compromise

Power players aren't timorous when it
comes to tackling criticism, but they shouldn't
be unguided missiles in responding.

EARLY EVERY MORNING, like clockwork, the
personal assistant of a high-profile CEO who is a client
of mine scans the Web for what was said about the boss,
looking especially for negative comments. When he finds
some of those comments, and a day rarely goes by when
he does not, he catalogs them and starting at 7 a.m. be-
gins to discuss what to do about the situation. Nothing?
A letter to the editor? A lawsuit? What?

As the digital age advances, it's getting easier for
people to assail one another. You have to be prepared for
that. You have to be prepared to deal with a world that's
becoming meaner, fouler, and more venal.

Before blogging became fashionable, there was something known as flaming. Flaming essentially meant rude
comments about a person that would be posted on various

bulletin boards on the Internet. Corporate executives were especially vulnerable. Anyone could say what he or she wished about them and their companies' products. Vicious rumors would be spread about people's personal lives.

The blogosphere and the freewheeling Internet chat forums that embrace virtually every subject under the sun have multiplied opportunities to escalate and sustain personal and professional attacks on people, particularly those who have some prominence.

What counts here is not the content or severity of the attacks but the way one handles them. Precisely because the blogosphere has created an open, unfiltered megaphone for anyone with a computer and a modem, a striking characteristic of contemporary times is an unseemly incivility.

Winners are never surprised by these assaults. I once had the privilege of being with the late J. Peter Grace, a scion of the eponymous company, when he received news of a particularly venal bit of criticism. I asked why he seemed so composed. "Such criticism doesn't make any difference to me," Grace said. "I'm in the arena; I chose to be there. I live by my convictions."

That was as sturdy a statement of personal integrity as I've ever heard, but I sometimes wonder how he would have reacted to being vilified in the blogosphere, which of course hadn't arrived while Grace was around.

Now that anyone can start a blog—and it often seems that everyone has one—the opportunities for unmonitored and unfiltered name-calling on the Web have increased exponentially. In the cause of greater transparency, CEOs and corporations are opening themselves up more and more online to the scrutiny of the world in a way that's never been done before. They are making themselves vulnerable to the vicissitudes of life and the malevolence of others. Sites such as Gawker.com and Jossip.com traffic in unsubstantiated news; they will put anything out there to attract more eyeballs, and it is going to get worse.

If you want to find out what's in the blogosphere about your company, visit blog-focused search engines such as Blogpulse.com and Technorati.com. Those engines allow you to search by keywords.

When Jessica Coen, an editor at Gawker, left to take a better-paying job at VanityFair.com, she admitted in her farewell note to readers that she had no regrets about having been mean and nasty about people on the site. Implicit in her statement was the certainty that few people can afford to sue Web sites that put out outrageous falsehoods.

Sarah Murray of the *Financial Times*, who follows Internet-related issues, says that for companies that are worried about how consumers and activists view their business practices, new channels of communication such as blogs "present a fresh challenge, undermining a traditional command-and-control approach to corporate communication and reputation management."

"The Internet has long been a powerful medium for anticorporate messages," Murray says. "Moreover, material posted on these Web sites often remains accessible via search engines long after it is first published."

It is getting easier and easier to post data on the Internet. At one time you had to be a techie to handle the intricacies of uploading something onto a Web site. Videos were difficult to upload. Now technology has made matters so convenient that not only can you create your own blog within minutes, you can post videos on sites such as YouTube with hardly any filtering. Several studies have shown that each year about 4 million posts that attack corporations appear on Web sites. For the business community, that's an unseen enemy out there.

Not only has the Internet become a gossip mill, but it's frequently used to damage or destroy someone's reputation. Successful entrepreneurs are often the target of such campaigns. Dolly Lenz, one of this country's most accomplished real estate brokers, is a case in point. Lenz, who works with Prudential Douglas Elliman, is the one to whom celebrities and other high-fliers turn when they want to buy showcase homes in New York. Her clients include Barbra Streisand and Bruce Willis.

Some of Lenz's rivals started a whispering campaign about her, and it moved to the Web. Ugly rumors were put out, the worst being that Lenz, a plucky cancer survivor, was dying and therefore her clients should take their business elsewhere. None of the rumors were true, and Lenz wasn't one to take things lying down. She conducted her own reputation management campaign, one that proved so effective that she got even more clients than before. Now Lenz typically makes $6 million or $7 million every year.

Like Dolly Lenz, you have to learn how to be the man or woman in the arena. No matter how difficult things get, no matter how challenging things become, you have to stand up for what you think is right. You have to do the right thing. You have to say to yourself, "I know how to overcome malevolence; I know how to overcome bad times; I know how to overcome difficulties."

How can technology help you take the heat? I'm not suggesting that you do something illegal or unethical. Not long ago, when unfavorable articles about Hewlett-

Packard started appearing in newspapers, certain board directors authorized wiretaps of employees' phones and the monitoring of their Web usage. The company's chairman resigned in the wake of the scandal and later was indicted.

There are people out there who will try to use information against you. There is no question about it. You have to be alert.

One of my clients employs a man who calls or writes those who make negative comments about him or his company. In those face-to-face, in-person meetings or in their telephone calls, the offender usually apologizes.

However, most of us cannot afford the pressure or the time to do such bird-dogging. So what should we do, ignore it? Maybe.

Always remember that it takes many repeated impressions to have a view or an idea take hold in the public mind. One impression will not do it.

I know a fine fellow who used to run a very important pharmaceutical company. There were whispers that he was having an affair with a woman who worked with him. One afternoon, he received a phone call from his wife. She was confronting him with what she'd just read on a Web gossip site.

"It's just not true," the executive told her.

"But it's here in cyberspace for everybody to see, and it's embarrassing to us as a couple, at the very least," the wife said.

The executive had to defend himself vigorously in cyberspace against the accusation of marital infidelity. However, he was perhaps a bit too stout on his own behalf, defending himself so aggressively that he ended up highlighting his personal problem in people's minds. He should have posted one straightforward statement refuting the allegations, and that would have been it. Instead, he was constantly answering and answering accusations. He wound up losing his job.

My company has well over 50,000 citations on the Web, and I've got over 300,000 hits associated with my name. My professional life has been laid out there for everybody to see. Do I examine each entry? Of course not. If I did, I'd never have time to do anything else. But I'm assuming that some people out there probably do "research" on my company and me. If they could, they probably would use the information against me, or maybe they'd use it for me, or maybe they'd use it to gauge who I am and what my company is about and what it is going to do.

I know that some of the entries I have seen pertaining to my business and myself are plain wrong. If I spent my life correcting stuff on the Web, that is all I would do, and so I don't do that. What I do is focus on positive things that are not on the Web. For example, if I deliver a speech, I try to find ways to get its text on the Web. If I receive an award or some other type of recognition, I try to get that posted on the Web. If I'm part of an organization and we have a photograph that reflects something that we did, I try to get that on the Web. In these cases I hope the good stuff will overcome the stuff that is wrong or not so good and will help the company. At the very least, there will be fewer untruths out there.

This gets to the question of what it means to have your own Web site and, if you do, how to keep it current and interesting. Your Web site should not simply be a bulletin board for personal or company announcements. It's important to sustain interactivity. That means inviting your readers to respond and addressing the issues they raise in a truthful, cordial fashion. Under no circumstances should you use a Web site, particularly a corporate one, to get into mudslinging.

The world is littered with "Web masters" who are supposed to excel at creating statements about companies or people that get the correct image out there. Those individuals use color, graphics, links to other Web sites, and dozens of other devices to tell a story.

However, if there arc several hundred mentions about you, it is those mentions, not your Web site, no matter how well it is constructed, that will draw attention. That is not to suggest that you should not put up a superb site for your company or for yourself personally, but "having a Web presence" is a misunderstood tool; it isn't as important as having open networks of information.

If you intend to be a public person, your real goal should be to get proper packages of data out there for all to see: your speeches, an article, a time you were quoted. All these things will create the impression people will take away. More and more, merely having a Web presence counts for less and less.

You need to amplify your channels of communications in a manner that is transparent. Elliot Schrage, the head of communications and public affairs at Google, says that it's important for companies to be consistent in what they put out on the Web. "Companies that try to maintain postures that are different from their corporate behavior will be natural candidates for scrutiny and derision," he told the *Financial Times*. However, that paper's Sarah Murray notes, although many companies have policies on how to engage with traditional media and even on blogging, few have in-house rules about the sort of instant response required by bloggers and social networks.

If you don't want to be a public person, if you want to fly under the radar, is it wise not to pay attention to this?

You must pay attention because no matter how wealthy or well connected you are, reputations can be fragile and vulnerable to malicious undermining, particularly on the Web. I have two lists: the wealthiest people in the world and the wealthiest families in the world. For the most part, none of those people appear in *Forbes* or *Fortune*, and nearly all avoid the limelight.

However, with simple research on the names and through databases, I can create a file of some heft on each of those individuals or families. Thus they have to take steps to protect themselves.

Every holiday season I try to vacation at a terrific resort called Le Semmana in St. Maarten in the Caribbean. There is a man there who comes to work by boat every morning. He deposits his outboard near shore, drops anchor, and comes to the beach. At the end of the day he reverses the procedure and goes home.

There is no way to track this man, right? Wrong.

This person, who seeks privacy, has dozens of mentions about him on the Web. Vacationers have written plenty about him. The local newspaper has a file that can be accessed and Googled. His quest for a private life has not worked.

If you know how to search, you will be able to get almost any information you wish about an individual or a company. That includes tax records and divorce settlements even if they supposedly have been sealed. We can find out if there are liens against people with whom we would like to do business. We can even learn their sexual preferences.

My friend L. Paul Bremer, who was President George W. Bush's first viceroy in Iraq after American troops liberated that Middle Eastern country from the tyranny of Saddam Hussein, is someone who understands the uses and value of technology.

"The Internet is complicated," Bremer says. "It is useful for research. But it is fraught with danger. I suppose it's an empowering technology, but also a democratizing technology. As a CEO, I can now do my research myself. That still means one has to exercise caution about what's out there. The Senate Armed Services Committee Web site may be reliable, but not every site is."

A question that I've been asked for some years is whether you should go back and reshape all the stuff that is out there on you on the Web. My answer is no, simply because you do not have time to do that.

As a power player, whether you're a CEO or are about to become one or aspire to be one, how do you protect yourself against malevolence that is abetted by technology?

One way to do it is through association. You must try to associate yourself with people, causes, and institutions that are not negative. You should try to look for citations about yourself or people who have made citations about you that are positive and good and then try to highlight those citations in your company literature or blog. Of course, in this age of hyperscrutiny, you also don't want to seem immodest. There is no need to list every award you've received since kindergarten, but you should post the citations that fortify your professional credentials. At the very least, such postings establish a public record of your career and accomplishments.

Blogging doesn't have to be all negative. You can generate positive dialogue on the Web, particularly if you think you've been wronged. Positive language that reflects on who you are is a huge factor in the way you are interpreted. One word can make a big difference. You have to be very careful about what you put on the Web.

That requires constant vigilance. Companies have to respond proactively to assaults on their reputation. Sarah Murray advises companies to manage their online conversations better. "Companies that enter the blogosphere need to be prepared to post even the most critical comments about their brands, products, or behavior. They also need to respond quickly and with the right voice. Communications that come across like press releases will attract criticism," she says.

You have to understand that it's a brave new world out there. If you are unwilling to adapt to it, you are going to lose everything that is dear and near to you. You need to be prepared to suffer losses, humiliation, and embarrassment. Also, you had better understand the rules of getting up off the canvas and coming back without compromising your values like the great boxer Jim Braddock, who was portrayed by Russell Crowe in *Cinderella Man*.

Braddock showed that maintaining a sense of dignity and a sense of oneself is extremely important. When you are changing your career or changing your job or attempting a comeback, you tend to think, "Am I really worth it? Did I do something wrong; is there a problem here?" You should not think that. You should say to yourself, "I am who I am. I've got talent; I've got spirit; I've got enthusiasm. I can do this."

After you've resolved to take the heat, you need to rely on your friends and your networks, and, very important, you have to rely on the special skills you bring to the party. Most people have a special skill, and that makes a difference.

I remember going to big Fortune 20 companies when I left Hill & Knowlton and was planning to start my own communications company. Some longtime clients gave me the cold shoulder; but most, such as Procter & Gamble and the Ford Motor Company, continued their relationship with me. That gave me the confidence to think that I was providing a valuable service and that by continuing their relationship with me, those companies actually got me to increase the value I was bringing them. I never compromised myself or my values to sustain their trust in me.

Those values certainly include my faith and my family life. My wife, Jan, had a huge career with Estée Lauder and Revlon and later with Marshall Fields, but she gave up that flourishing career to help me. Therefore, I couldn't let her down. That was a big thing.

My faith in God has been extremely important. I know it is not popular to talk about God these days, but when under assault, I had a choice of saying that I am going to be an agnostic and it is all going against me or I am going to reach to a higher level and try to do the right thing from a religious point of view. I've always done the latter. That has been a big thing for me, and the strength that it gives a person is extraordinary.

I want to end this chapter by referring to a man who certainly knew how to take the heat. Back in 1969, when I was a novice in the field of communications and public relations, the newly elected president, Richard Milhous Nixon, offered me advice that proved incalculably important. It came in the form of a very simple test on how to be happy and fulfilled.

Nixon asked me to write on a blank piece of paper the three or four qualities in life that were important to me: family, wealth, health, travel, friends, and so on. Then the president urged me to put the paper aside for a few days and after some reflection look at it again.

You see, Nixon believed correctly that we all tell ourselves what we would like to hear and not what is really accurate. Once you arrive at a short list of qualities that are really important to you, Nixon said, "make sure that whatever you do every day in your life in the coming years gives you those qualities."

His insight was simple but powerful. From the time you are awake and functioning, you have to acquire the qualities you believe are important to you. That eventually will make you happy. When you are really happy and balanced and at peace with the world, the issue of power takes on a totally different and more profound dimension.

I have taken this "test" every year since 1969. Other than an enduring emphasis on putting my family first, the other priorities have changed over the years. For example, I used to think I was invincible and would live forever. Now I know that good health counts. I know that the proximity of special friends can elicit more well-being than can any amount of recreational travel.

Try that test. It works, and by diligently using the ideas in this book, you will be on the road to becoming truly powerful and mastering the elements around you. You will reach greater heights in whatever it is you seek. You will have mastered that zone where emotions, ambitions, expectations, and technological change converge.

7

Keep Focusing
on Your Strengths

*Focusing on your strengths means
knowing yourself and your adversaries.*

A. D. "PETE" CORRELL, the former CEO of
Georgia-Pacific and one of the most technologically savvy
executives in the world, once defined the difference
between winners and losers for me, saying that, "Successful
people have compassion and understanding and the
ability to listen before they act. They know how to bring
people together as a team. Unsuccessful people like to
grandstand, blurt out opinions, and see themselves as the
beginning and the end."

I saw this up close when Correll, a brilliant strategist,
transformed Georgia-Pacific into one of the hot financial
players of the decade.

Time and again, Correll listened and actually took
notes. Over and over, he heard the executives under him
call for attention. Painstakingly, Correll committed all he
had to notes and spreadsheets.

Correll was criticized at coffee breaks for not taking action. He was derided after hours for not moving quickly enough. He experienced humiliation. But did he?

What was Correll doing? He was gathering consensus. He sacrificed his own ego in the short term for long-term gain. This man used every working moment and involved every element of technology—e-mails, Google research, and much more—to reach his goal. Only he and his trusted adviser Sheila Weidman-Farley knew what was taking place and how the technology was being used.

The end result was that everyone won: the shareholders, the employees, the customers, and the top managers who had scorned Pete Correll because they thought he should have done more. Correll knew that one of his strengths was the ability to listen to others and grasp every nuance in a conversation. He didn't care what people thought he was doing. He understood that a big part of a CEO's job is to figure out what is on people's minds. He didn't mind that in the perception of some he projected ennui or inaction. Correll knew that at the end of the day he would be able to synthesize issues and produce a workable solution to the problem at hand.

Correll was called on by the United Nations to contribute ideas to its Earth Summit that was held in Rio de Janeiro in June 1992. In recognition of his commitment to environmental protection, Theodore W. Kheel, the venerable labor lawyer who had been enlisted by the UN to spread awareness of the summit, gave Correll an award. It consisted of a limited-edition print titled Earth Pledge that the famous artist Robert Rauschenberg had created at Kheel's behest.

Indeed, Kheel's involvement with the UN pointed to the way he focused on a special strength. He'd long been interested in the environment, but it was not until the journalist Pranay Gupte suggested to Kheel that his engagement with the Earth Summit would be welcomed by the UN that the lawyer obtained an entrée. Kheel and Gupte had known each other since the time when the latter was a reporter at *The New York Times*, and the two had kept in touch over the years. Gupte knew that Kheel was highly skilled at obtaining publicity and that the painter Rauschenberg was among his high-profile clients. He also knew that Kheel was getting restless in his semiretirement.

At that time, Gupte was informally advising the summit's secretary general, Maurice F. Strong, a Canadian businessman long active in global environmental issues. He brought Strong and Kheel together, and then Kheel formed a committee that raised millions of dollars from the private sector in support of the Earth Summit. Kheel sold Rauschenberg's prints for $50,000 apiece to corporations. Some of that money was used to start an independent newspaper on the environment and sustainable development, *Earth Times*, which Gupte ran from 1991 to 2003.

His involvement with the Earth Summit was a new career of sorts for Ted Kheel. He was nearly eighty at the time. By focusing on his strengths, which, besides being knowledgeable about the media, included an encyclopedic acumen for dealing with developmental issues, Kheel soon became a stellar figure in the global environmental movement. Not bad for a New York icon who very nearly had retired from practicing law.

Like Ted Kheel, Ali Cromie, a woman in Australia, jump-started a new career by focusing on her strengths. She's a New Zealander by birth but moved to Sydney in her teens. Within a few years Cromie became one of Australia's top business journalists. She won every award there was to win. From print, Cromie moved to television, where she also excelled.

At that point journalism began to lose its allure for Cromie. She wanted to do something else, but what? Because of her celebrity, Cromie could have gotten almost any kind of job she wanted in the lucrative world of investment banking or in securities. She took stock of her strengths and came to the conclusion that one of her key assets was an ability to size up people, analyze their background, establish their integrity, and assess how they performed in their profession. Should she accept an offer to join a high-end corporate executive recruiting firm? Cromie sensed that Australian corporations increasingly were looking to retain board directors, especially independent ones who would be less susceptible to blandishments and bounties from CEOs.

Cromie decided to start her own company for recruiting directors. The company, the Rigour Group, was successful from the get-go, a testimony to Cromie's determination to keep focusing on her strengths. To add to her repertoire, she's now studying for a law degree, which she feels will enable her to widen her business prospects. (Earlier, while she was a journalist, Cromie obtained an MBA.)

As I see it, Ali Cromie's case offers several pointers: You should be good at figuring out who you are, what you want to do, what you want to be, and how are you going to get there. Because of the extensive contacts she gained through journalism, Cromie knew whom to alert about her new business.

There is an intuitive sense about decision making that very smart people have. They're born with it. Of course, you can get training in the discipline of decision making: how to analyze the elements of a business situation and come up with options for action. However, this is an intuitive sense that comes naturally to some of the most successful CEOs I know, such as Jeffrey Immelt of General Electric. When that critical moment comes, intuition comes into play and a decision is made.

How does one know that this process is natural or intuitive? It's a function of cognitive recognition. It's the way one's brain works. One simply knows when a eureka moment has arrived. It's a bit like that old TV commercial for the Ford Motor Company in which a lightbulb would be turned on when a good idea occurred to the person on the screen. For example, Immelt sensed how important the question of global warming was going to be. He sensed that big business had better join the environmental movement not as a cause but because developing cleaner technology would not only lessen pollution but also make profits for companies in the long run.

Like Immelt, Switzerland's Stephan Schmidheiny, whose family owns the world's biggest cement manufacturing business, among other things, understood that big business could make production changes relatively swiftly because of its access to resources. Schmidheiny helped start the World Business Council on Sustainable Development, a nonpartisan organization based in Geneva; its members now include practically every major company in the world. Both Schmidheiny and Immelt possessed strong intuition and an ability to think ahead, and each in his own way focused on those strengths when dealing with environmental issues.

I know a big-time financial executive who always figures out at least two steps that will follow virtually every decision he makes. Whenever he makes a decision, he says either *a* is going to happen or *b* is going to happen. He already has thought about the first step. Then he says, If *a* happens, here are the next two things that are going to happen. This guy has thought ahead probably thirty or forty minutes—not hours, not days, but minutes. He is way ahead of anybody who is trying to come to grips with something that happens in an instant. He knows that one of his strengths lies in projecting scenarios, and so he focuses on that. He takes out a yellow legal pad and diagrams a decision.

Henry Schadt, who used to run Cummins Engine and is now a major player at Warburg Pincus, thought months and years ahead. He gathered every bit of research he could find and applied it to models that no one had thought of. He built one of the greatest companies in the world.

There are certain strengths that you must build as a power player. One of them is the ability to do exhaustive research on your clients. The tools are there to do this, and what used to take days can now be handled in minutes. By knowing our strengths and building on them in a hypercompetitive world, we can be more effective. You need to learn how to block out your weaknesses, prune them, and drive steadily from your strengths. That takes an enormous amount of discipline.

Not long ago, my colleagues and I were scheduled to meet a prospective client who needed some persuasion to commit himself to a hundred-million-dollar project. We had less than three hours to prepare for the meeting. Before the afternoon meeting I took my colleagues for lunch at the Park Avenue Café, which is not far from our office in Manhattan. It's a beautiful place, and the food is pretty good. They have very good oysters from all parts of the world.

We sat down at this lunch to discuss how we were going to approach the client. We had brought some files on the man. We knew everything there was to know about him. We knew where he went to school, what kind of a group he brought in to celebrate his birthday, where he lived, how much he paid in taxes, and whether he had a police record (he did not).

In such exercises we do a thing called "words and phrases." We go into somebody's past and take all the stories that have been written about that person, let's say Johnny Jones. Let's also say that Jones has more than 3,000 references to him on Google. We go through them all. We ask, "What words and phrases have been used to describe Johnny Jones? What does that mean?" Often the words and phrases are very positive; sometimes they are negative. Often they point to a trend. Sometimes they point to an inclination. We'll seize on that and say, "How do we now take that and turn it so that it can be helpful to us in a meeting?" I don't think that a lot of people do that.

We knew that the client we were to see that afternoon happened to like a certain rock group and hired it to play at his birthday each year.

When my team walked into this man's office later that afternoon, the first thing I asked was how the rock group was doing. Immediately, he was on our turf rather than we being on his. When we left, I gave him two CDs by the group. We would not have been able to accomplish that if we had not done the research. That's the first point.

The second point is that we knew what our real goal was. We did not show that goal right away. We let the man enter into a discussion with us about several points that did not relate to our real goal but led to it. He actually got to our real goal before we did, and then it became his idea rather than ours.

It was a wonderful way to get this guy to make a huge decision and commit about $100 million to a significant operation. We did it because we conducted our research—our due diligence—ahead of time. And we did not have much time to do it. We were able to do it because we understood where to go on the tech map. We used our databases; those databases are known to many, but people don't take the time to get into them.

I knew that among my strengths were two things: the ability to do timely research and the ability to be patient in a conversation. As I advance in my career and understand what is effective, I bring those strengths to every project I undertake. I don't waste time experimenting. I know what works and what doesn't. This is where experience kicks in, as does intuition. One gains more self-confidence as one grows older, I think, although I must acknowledge that an unending run of setbacks can be disheartening to most people. Be that as it may, power players must develop fortitude.

One of the smartest men I've ever met, A. Robert Abboud, understood this. Abboud was a banker at First Chicago. His career also included stints in oil and gas, private investment, and foreign affairs. Whenever he was to attend a meeting, Abboud would wait until the room was just about full but not totally full. He then would walk into the doorway and would stand there for a moment, with nobody else around him. He was a short man, impeccably tailored. He exuded power.

Inevitably, someone would say, "Bob, how are you?"

The entire room would turn toward him. Abboud would salute and say, "Let's start." He really got control of the room by doing that.

Of course, well before he had made that grand entrance, Bob Abboud would know exactly who everyone in attendance was. He would have done his research. His colleague, another very smart banker named Robert Richly, would have told him about the top four or five people he should meet and why. Richly would have done his research on databases such as Lexis-Nexis and Bloomberg. Moreover, Abboud would have his priorities clearly etched in his mind. When he walked into a meeting, he would say to himself and sometimes to his audience, "There are five things I have to do; I cannot leave the room until I've done those five things."

Abboud showed his strength by getting others to focus on him. However, the key thing here is that, grand entrances aside, he always came prepared for every meeting. He also made sure that he listened to all points of view and that his mind wasn't made up on any issue until he'd heard all the sides. Abboud was also careful to accord the proper respect to his colleagues.

He took nothing for granted.

In doing all this, he mirrored an idea that was given to me many years by the head of the United Automobile Workers (UAW), Walter Reuther. The legendary Reuther was a veteran of many negotiations, and one day I asked him about the key to his success.

Reuther smiled and said: "In my negotiations, I always keep one cherry in my pocket. I give it to the people at the last second. They feel better about the fact I've won the negotiation. The Japanese will tell you they never want to win 100 percent—we'll take 95 percent and give the other side 5 percent."

That is another way of saying that you should always be magnanimous. Power players can show their strength by yielding a little.

I'd like to narrate one more story here. It deals with the popular product called Gatorade. I helped launch Gatorade. Here is how it happened. The launch was interesting, but it was pedestrian. What is really interesting, I think, is how Gatorade got to the point where it could be launched.

The corporation that I was to lead, Hill & Knowlton, had an account with a company called Stokely-Van Camp that was based in Indianapolis. It was a great company at that time, run by a man named Alfred Stokely. It was a family company, and the head of marketing was a man named Hank Warren, and there was also a man named Cliff Marquart, who was Warren's deputy and who was to oversee the Gatorade brand.

I was at company headquarters one day, and all of a sudden Alfred Stokely got a telephone call from somebody who was at the Indianapolis airport. The caller was a man named Dr. James Robert Cade. The doctor was passing through Indianapolis on the way from Chicago back to his home state of Florida; he was changing planes in Indianapolis. He called Stokely and said he had a product called Gatorade that he had been using with the Florida Gators football team, and he wondered if Stokely would have any interest in the product. Stokely was a risk taker who recognized an interesting idea when he heard one and knew how to take advantage of it. Warren was every bit his equal in that regard. Both men knew how to focus on their respective strengths.

Warren sent a car to the Indianapolis airport, and Dr. Cade came to a meeting in Indianapolis with Stokely-Van Camp; Alfred Stokely bought the product that very day. Dr. Cade later sued the company because he felt the organization bought the product unfairly and took advantage of him. He was also going to sue Florida University, and Florida University sued Stokely-Van Camp as well. But Gatorade was born. That resulted in an extraordinary set of experiences for me in which I introduced Gatorade to tennis stars like Jimmy Connors, Broadway stars like Yaphet Kotto, and the National Football League, Major League Baseball, and many more groups.

What is the message here? The same points that started this chapter. Stokely and Warren were inquisitive, focused, and determined. They succceded not just because they met Bob Cade but because they had done their research and knew what the public was thirsting for. When Cade arrived on their doorstep, it was a slam dunk.

My experience doing that taught me all kinds of lessons. First, it taught me that the heroes who are our athletes today sometimes really are not heroes after all; they are simply men and women who are very skilled and can do something exquisite that people will pay to watch. Second, it taught me all about promotion. I'll never forget Hank Stram, who was the coach of the Kansas City Chiefs, sitting across the aisle from me on a plane in Florida. He said to me, "Look, I really like you, kid. I'll promote Gatorade for you." That was a very generous thing for Stram to do. He didn't have to do it, but he did, and it had an enormous impact.

I'll never forget serving hot Gatorade one very cold day in December to the Los Angeles Rams in Minnesota and cold Gatorade to the Minnesota Vikings, who were playing the Rams that day. The idea behind the hot Gatorade was to make it easier for the Rams, who played more often in a warmer climate, to move. The cold Gatorade was for the Vikings because they were tough. At halftime the Rams were winning the game, and a big Rams guard named Tom Mack, who had played earlier for the University of Michigan, came rushing over to me. Although I'm a big guy, he lifted me up on his shoulder and said, "This is the guy who is winning the game for us."

I said, "This is fantastic, and Mr. Mack, it's going to take a lot more than that."

In any event, the Minnesota Vikings won the game. I'll also never forget a Viking end named Henderson (number 80) catching a pass over his shoulder in the last few seconds. The Rams were fit to be tied and looked for a reason why they had lost the game; they blamed it on Gatorade and on me. Needless to say, I could not get back into the Rams locker room after the game.

Perspective—an important part of leadership and of winning—is a matter of understanding the environment you are in. Not long ago I took a client to meet Henry Kissinger. The client wanted to know about China. Kissinger graciously asked how much time the client could give him. The client had an assistant with him who was aware of his boss's importance and barked, "Thirty minutes, not a moment more. We have a critical meeting uptown."

Kissinger smiled and in a very relaxed manner said, "In that case we will start with the fifteenth century." Dr. Kissinger went on for twenty-eight minutes, delivering a tour-de-force lecture on China. The client and his assistant were awestruck. In the twenty-ninth minute Kissinger graciously said, "Good-bye."

The client knew at that moment that he should have stayed longer, but he couldn't. On Park Avenue outside Kissinger's office, the client looked at his assistant and asked, "Why did we only have thirty minutes?" The assistant, embarrassed, mumbled something. He later lost his job.

8

Keep Growing Your Network by Shaving It

There's no substitute for a powerful
network that embraces you and
even nurtures you. You cannot do it alone.

Henry Dormann is the editor and publisher
of *Leaders* magazine, a coffee table quarterly that features
CEOs and heads of state and is redolent of power.

Every morning Dormann sits at his desk on the
third floor of a building on East Fifty-Third Street in
Manhattan and opens a drawer at the right. The drawer is
jammed tight with three-by-five index cards that list the
top people in the world, the contacts Dormann has had
with each, background on each, and much more.

This is the Dormann Rolodex. It is invaluable, and it
has enabled Dormann to reach thousands of CEOs, heads
of state, foreign ministers, and others.

It has taken Dormann more than twenty years to
build his database. Today he supplements the index-card
treasure with one-line research summaries that enable
him to have still more data *before* he makes a contact.

As the day starts, Dormann starts to make calls and make money. It is phenomenal to see.

What accounts for his success? It is the database, but it is also the personal research he has compiled over decades that gives him an edge no one else can touch. In other words, Dormann is a power broker.

I've always been fascinated by this question: How do big-time politicians manage their Rolodexes? George H. W. Bush, who was the forty-first president of the United States, sends out Christmas cards to tens of thousands of people in virtually every country, and those are just the men and women he knows personally. Imagine how many more people he's shaken hands with during a long career in public life. The man who defeated him in the 1992 election, Bill Clinton, is reputed to have a photographic memory for names. For a politician, of course, knowing people translates into votes. Is it any wonder that Clinton has been one of the most successful politicians of our time?

Politicians sometimes are accused of "using" people, of dismantling alliances and discarding friendships when their purpose is served. There is, of course, some truth to that, but any successful politician will tell you that a certain amount of calibration is needed when it comes to supporters and constituents. The trick is to maintain an "up" list and a "down" list without alienating anyone.

Kamal Nath, India's minister of commerce and industry, knows this as well as anybody. He has been in politics since his student days, when he was one of that country's most prominent youth leaders. For nearly three decades Nath has been elected to the Lok Sabha, the lower house of India's parliament, each time with a big majority. A scion of a wealthy Calcutta industrial family,

Nath represents Chhindwara, a tribal region in central India, and one of the country's poorest areas. He's about the same age as Bill Clinton—sixty—and, like Clinton, Nath has a photographic memory for faces and names.

Nath's technique for dealing with the constantly growing number of names in his Rolodex is to keep creating new categories. For example, there's the environment category, which dates back to the early 1990s, when he was minister of the environment and led India's delegation to the Earth Summit in Rio de Janeiro. Now there's the trade category, not least because he leads developing countries in their negotiations with rich ones at the World Trade Organization in Geneva. Then there's a master list, and there's a special list of people with whom Nath needs to stay in constant contact, such as Prime Minister Manmohan Singh and the powerful Congress Party president Sonia Gandhi. It's all very sophisticated, and Nath has immediate access to more than 20,000 names in his PDA.

Like politicians, investment bankers depend on the people they know to make a living. Wall Street might as well be renamed Rolodex Street. In mergers and acquisitions, among other things, big deals often are made by tapping into a power player's informal network. Steven Rattner, founder of the equity firm the Quadrangle Group, is legendary for his Rolodex, prompting some of his rivals in the investment banking business to wonder whether there is *anyone* he doesn't know.

Similarly, journalists usually maintain formidable collections of contacts. Lionel Barber, the editor of the *Financial Times*, sometimes would tell me over lunch in New York, where he used to be based when he was that newspaper's U.S. editor, how carefully he cultivated contacts in the many countries to which he traveled as a foreign correspondent. *The New Yorker's* Seymour Hersh is reputed to possess a list of thousands of sources whom he can reach for his extraordinary investigative stories.

Most corporate executives do not have a network like those mentioned above. When you explore who has such networks in professions such as law and accounting, in the nonprofit world, and in local communities, the number is extremely low.

That's too bad. If people such as those knew how to network and whom to network with, their goals and aspirations would be achieved much more easily.

There is a wonderful hospital in New York, the nation's largest city, that does not understand how to leverage the relationships its board has or the ones it has with the people it spends money with: its suppliers. Instead, the hospital staff labors with the right intentions as it tries to raise money and build awareness of its skills and the creative powers it has.

It has an information technology department that should use its relationships with Oracle and IBM to generate more effective outreach. It has a blue chip board of directors, each member of which has a great personal list that could be placed into a database to be sliced and diced to help patients, doctors, nurses, the hospital's research staff, and many others.

Why doesn't the hospital do this? I don't know. It's something I've recommended for years, but somehow the bureaucracy gets in the way, and little, if anything, happens.

Perhaps this institution should take a look at how the chairperson of the American Red Cross strengthens her personal network. Bonnie McElveen-Hunter, who's also the CEO of Pace Communications, has been a networker all her life. She's been ambassador to Finland and has run several nonprofits. The common denominator in all those positions was her ability to develop networks. I recently got a firsthand look at how she manages her enormous network when McElveen-Hunter joined me for lunch at a private club in midtown Manhattan.

She showed up with two assistants who set up a laptop at a discreet distance from our lunch table. Each one had a cell phone and a BlackBerry. They were prioritizing her incoming messages and quietly signaling to her on her BlackBerry which messages she needed to respond to immediately. As it happened, one of those messages was from the White House, and McElveen-Hunter responded to it without making a fuss.

A power player knows the importance of developing networks. As Bonnie McElveen-Hunter demonstrated that afternoon, the trick is knowing how to manage them. In a seventeen- or eighteen-hour workday there are only so many people with whom you can stay in touch. In effect, your power network needs to change on a daily basis. That means you must prioritize: Who's currently essential to your business? What about former clients who might give you business again? Who do you keep on your holiday season card list and who do you eliminate?

I don't want to seem cynical or opportunistic about how power players should deal with people. I always say that you should try to remain close to your friends (and even closer to your enemies), including those in the business world. Keep your friends from ten or twenty years ago even though you may not be doing business with them any longer. Make sure you never take people totally off the list but realize as you go forward that you are going to be adding people constantly. Never totally cut yourself off from the people who were originally part of your network because they are often people you can count on if push comes to shove.

Here is an example from my life. There is man named Michael Calvert who was a city planner in Baltimore and is now one in Birmingham, Alabama. I've known Calvert for forty-five years. We used to be close business associates. Nowadays Calvert comes into my life maybe two or three times every few years, but I know if I ever ask him to help me, he will step forward because I've kept in touch with him informally. Is he part of my "active" network today? No, but I know I can count on him because I've made it a point to stay in touch with him, however infrequently. People appreciate that occasional surprise call or birthday card.

Young professionals should start developing such networks early in their careers. Look at Larry Page and Sergey Brin. In 1998 they were graduate students at Stanford University and had come up with a search engine. They asked one of their professors, Jeffrey Ullman, for guidance. Ullman invited an investor he knew, Ram Shriram, to come to his office to meet the two young men and test their product. The professor had kept in touch with Shriram since Shriram's time at Amazon.com. Now that he'd become a venture capitalist, all sorts of people wanted Shriram to back them. He left Professor Ullman's office without making a decision.

However, Page and Brin already had made him a part of their network. Two months after meeting Shriram, they called him. "I had no premonition of the things to come," he says. He became an angel investor and a board member in their new company, Google. He helped them with hiring. "Hire only 'A' people," Shriram would say to Page and Brin.

How does one identify "A" people? "I try to find out who their mothers are," Shriram says. "If they are raised well, they're more likely to make good citizens, employees, and entrepreneurs." Now, less than a decade after Page and Brin met Shriram, Google is a global company with tens of thousands of employees and market capitalization of more than $140 billion. Shriram, who heads his own company, continues to mentor young entrepreneurs in technology, advising them continually to strengthen their network of contacts no matter how successful they become.

Another person Page and Brin consulted was the management guru Ram Charan. I met Charan through Dun & Bradstreet and Bob Weissman many years ago, and now I hear from him once or twice a year, often with insights and suggestions that help my business. Because of who he is and what I learn from his talents, I recommend him to my clients whenever I can.

Like Larry Page and Sergey Brin, Kris Ramanathan, the chief operating officer of Netomat.com, benefited by maintaining a network in the financial and technology communities. Before joining Netomat full time, Ramanathan was the CEO of MemberTree.com, an Internet start-up. It helped "brick and mortar" communities such as professional societies, trade associations, and other not-for-profit groups use the Internet to strengthen and broaden their relationships. As the founder, Ramanathan raised seed funding for the company and established software programming and business development operations in the United States and India. Before MemberTree.

com, Ramanathan helped launch and then ran U.S. operations for Financial Models Company, Inc., an international software company based in Canada. FMC offered portfolio management software to institutional investment managers. His clients included some of the largest financial institutions in the world: Citibank, Barclays, Bankers Trust, Invesco, Janus, and UBS.

Ramanathan was similarly successful at MemberTree. com. "But after a while, I felt that technology was starting to pass me by," he told me. "Sometimes you need to create change in your professional life through some sort of turbulence." For Ramanathan, that turbulence consisted of taking a two-month sabbatical. He could afford to do that because his wife, Sujana Chandrasekhar, was a physician who could support the family.

Among those in his network was a man named E. S. Purandar Das, formerly a vice chairman at Merrill Lynch, who had developed a reputation for mentoring promising young people on Wall Street. Ramanathan had long sought his counsel, and the older man readily gave it to him.

I've experienced such magnanimity myself. When I was working in Chicago many years ago, there came a point when I was somewhat desperate in terms of figuring out what the future was going to be like. I didn't really have a picture of the future; I didn't really have a goal. I knew I had to go in to work every day. I had to produce enough to get a check that would take care of my family, and that was important. I wanted to put good food on the table, I wanted to have a pleasant time on the weekend, and I wanted to go to sporting events and the opera.

I had met a man named John M. Richman. He was chairman and CEO of Kraft, the cheese manufacturer. I called him, and he agreed to meet me at his office. From that fateful day onward, Richman took me under his wing and gave me a chance, not the least by giving the Kraft PR account to me.

Richman also taught me about the importance of growing one's professional and personal network. He and his wife, Priscilla, would host wonderful parties at their home, and Richman would invite me even though I was a very junior executive. One day, in my presence, Priscilla Richman asked her husband why I was being invited to all their parties, which were attended by A-list people.

"Oh, Pril," Richman said to his wife, "Bob's not on the A list. He's on *the list*."

Richman opened up the whole world of the future, and power, for me; he sketched a vision of what was possible. He would talk about much more than his corporation. He would discuss international affairs, talking about creating more prosperous and peaceful societies around the world.

As I look back on those years, I still cannot figure out what it was about me that made Richman take such a strong interest in developing my career. Perhaps it was chemistry, but I think that it might have been the fact that I always treated him with respect and deference. Just as I learned from Richman that you have to be very careful in using power, I learned that you have to be very careful when dealing with people in positions of power. You need to learn not to offend anybody because you want to be in a position to tap that power source again.

In my business, developing networks is an integral part of the game. My business contacts have value. A man came to my office recently and asked if I would call four important people on his behalf. I knew those people well, and knew I could get them on the phone immediately. I asked the visitor how much he was prepared to pay for my calls.

"Well, I'll give you $5,000" the man said.

I told him that I wanted $25,000 to initiate those four phone calls.

"That's awfully expensive for four telephone calls," the man said.

"You can't do it without me," I replied.

"You mean you can just sit there now and make the four calls, and I give you $25,000?" my visitor said.

"That's how it's going to work," I said.

"But it's just four calls," he said.

"If you only want to make one call, I'll charge you $10,000, but the bottom line is that you can't make the calls and I can," I said.

Sometimes you have to be strong and firm with people. In that case I was.

No one knows how to deal with people better than Klaus Schwab. His Rolodex can put that of George H. W. Bush or Bill Clinton or even Kamal Nath to shame. In fact, for nearly four decades Schwab has made an institution out of networking.

That institution is the World Economic Forum, best known for the annual meeting that it organizes in the Swiss ski resort of Davos. Schwab, a Swiss-German, holds doctorates in engineering and economics and has taught management and public policy at the University of Geneva. He started the organization in 1971 as a way of gathering a number of his European friends to brainstorm on economic issues while also having fun, that is, as long as they liked to ski.

The annual gathering at Davos became so popular that Schwab soon found himself having to contend with thousands of applications for invitations. Because Davos is a small place, no more than 3,000 people can be accommodated. The World Economic Forum bills itself as an independent international organization "committed to improving the state of the world by engaging leaders in partnerships to shape global, regional and industry agendas." In addition to Davos, Schwab organizes annual gatherings in various parts of the world. If you aren't on his invitation list, as far as professional society is concerned, you can be deemed irrelevant.

I've been attending the Davos meetings almost since they were established, and I never cease to be amazed by Schwab's skill at putting people together. He has a big heart and would like to include everyone who wants to come, but his staff, which is responsible for the overall organization of the event, works hard to pare the list of invitees.

That's one way to handle your network, of course: trimming it without sentiment.

To some degree, we all need to be dispassionate about our contacts. However, for the true power player, networks are grown by smartly paring back those who no longer matter in your line of work.

Frank Stanton, the former president of CBS, who died in 2006, was a master at this. As Stanton advanced in years, he realized that he could not see everybody as often as he had as a young man. Instead, he wrote to people he wanted to keep close to once or twice a year but otherwise focused on those who would move the ball ahead for him and his causes. That is what the superlawyer Ted Kheel does too, revving up his massive Rolodex in service of the environment. (He's well past ninety now, but is wonderfully assisted by his foundation's executive director, Leslie Hoffman.)

Reverend Robert H. Schuller, who ran the Crystal Cathedral in Orange County, California, is another example. Schuller has touched millions, and millions feel that they have good and direct personal relationships with him. Schuller wanted it that way so that he could spread his message of peace and love to as many people as possible. However, he always knew that he couldn't reach millions or even thousands personally. Therefore, he has used technology and databases for his ministry to reach people around the world with communications that mean something to them and that are driven by Dr. Schuller and the symbols he has chosen to be associated with: the White House, the Wailing Wall, the Elysées Palace, and the Kremlin.

True power players know how to use symbols to extend their networks. Those symbols bring into one's sphere everyone who is associated with them. For example, if you associate yourself with your university, you have the potential of being associated with everyone who ever attended that school. If you associate yourself with a charity, the same thing is true.

I served as a director of a great organization, the American Red Cross, for nearly a decade. There isn't a day that I don't think about the Red Cross and all the good things it does. And I know that if I need to, I can reach out to others, such as Bonnie McElveen-Hunter, who have been associated with the Red Cross for many years for help and support.

For a power player, cultivating people is an ongoing task. There are different ways to do that. One method is to mingle actively in circles where fellow professionals move. That means attending benefits and other events that traditionally attract people on the move. Another method is to exude such confidence and charisma that people are attracted to you. Still another tactic is to do both.

New York–based Pallavi Shah is a master networker who needs to know exactly what is where and who is who at every moment. That's the case because of the nature of her unusual business, which involves organizing high-luxury tours to exotic parts of the world for CEOs and other well-heeled people. Formerly a PR executive for a major airline, Shah decided some years ago that she possessed such a sparkling network that it could launch her into being an independent entrepreneur. So she launched a company called Our Personal Guest, which has become one of the most successful ventures of its kind.

"Over the years I have gathered tens of thousands of names from all over the world, and the dilemma that I wrestle with a lot is how to pare my network," Shah says. "Technology has made it easier to maintain a network. But that same technology overloads you. So who do you shave off your network? You never know when someone in a network can help you."

Shah gets more than 500 e-mails a day. "Communications and technology are taking away discretionary time to do discretionary networking. I am way, way behind in my acknowledgments," she says. "So now I keep in close touch mostly with those people who are directly related to my business. I call it my judicious fit. It's not that I let my other contacts lapse. But more and more I find myself in a situation where they get in touch. And then it's as if there never was a gap in our association."

"I believe it's possible to reignite a relationship no matter how much time has lapsed. I get calls from people I haven't seen in thirty years," Shah says. "My tone is always welcoming. I give out the vibe that I appreciate being remembered. I seldom take umbrage over the fact that so and so disappeared for a decade. Maybe that's why I never seem to lose anyone as a friend."

We should all be so lucky.

9

Seek Acclaim
but Practice Humility

*Be strong in your actions and humble in
your heart. Sic transit gloria mundi.*

Visitors to my office on Park Avenue or my
home in Connecticut sometimes express surprise that
neither place has an "I am" room.

An I am room is one where many people I know
display their honors, accolades, and awards. They display
photographs of themselves with presidents and movie
stars. They display trophies. They display "tombstones."
the special Lucite plaques that investment banks give
to team members of a deal that closes successfully. An
I am room doesn't have to be an entire chamber filled
with recognitions; it can be a vestibule with an "ego wall"
decorated with photographs.

Whenever I see an I am room, I wonder why people
bother. Shouldn't an individual's accomplishments speak
for themselves? I think it's far more important for a person to stay grounded in his or her own self-confidence. In

my office you will find only pictures of my family. In the final analysis, only one's family truly matters.

I think humility is a very important part of this. There are a lot of people whose egos become bigger than they should be; they often believe their own press. That is a big mistake. Everybody puts his or her trousers on one leg at a time. For a power player, it's important to be humble enough to reach out to the shoeshine boy as well as the CEO. In fact, sometimes it's more important to reach out to the shoeshine boy so that the CEO sees that you're a person of the people, a person who's generous, who's humble, who's willing to do outreach.

I've been privileged to encounter men and women of great distinction who also possessed humility. One such person is Bill Moyers, the broadcaster. Another is Father Theodore Hesburgh, formerly head of the University of Notre Dame, my alma mater.

I first met Father Hesburgh when I was a freshman. I'd gone to Notre Dame mainly because my older brother, John, had graduated from there. I still remember the day my brother and father took me to the campus in South Bend, Indiana, not far from our hometown of Columbus, Ohio. My dormitory room—Number 401—was on the fourth floor of Breen Philips Hall. When my brother and father left, I went to the window to watch them as they headed toward the car. I said to myself, "This is it. I'm on my own. I have to take on life all by myself." It was a terrifying thought, yet in a strange way I understood instinctively that I had to get my game together in terms of courage and go forward.

Father Hesburgh wasn't just a Holy Cross priest who ran a large university. He was a man who believed in civil rights, justice, and social encouragement—all the things we should hold dear in American society—and championed those ideas at the federal level and globally while being the head of the university. What impressed me most about Father Hesburgh, however, wasn't so much his idealism and activism as his humility and accessibility. Whether it was a cafeteria worker or a powerful politician, he would deal with people in the same manner: with the utmost courtesy and a willingness to listen. He always made other people feel that he cared about them. I learned from Father Hesburgh that if you occupy a position of power and prominence, it's wise to wield that influence quietly by hearing what others have to say rather than by imposing your own views, however strongly held. I think that one reason he won over so many people to the civil rights movement was his ability to be completely at ease with even those who harbored extreme views or felt antagonism toward him.

In my last year at Notre Dame I met Ara Parseghian, who was already a famous football coach. When he was at Northwestern University, his team beat Notre Dame four times in four tries. Notre Dame hired him away in 1964. I was sitting in the college refectory when Parseghian came in and joined some of us who were dining. We all had a meal together, and he talked about what was important to him in life. He said excellence was really important. He said you should go as far as your potential can take you. He talked about the importance of honesty; he talked about the importance of loyalty; he talked about the importance of fair dealing; he talked about the importance of keeping a balance in your life, never going too far in any single direction. He never talked about football.

Parseghian's remark about the importance of balance in one's life has stayed with me. I've seen so many people who overcompensate. They spend too much time on business and too little time with their families. They spend so much time getting angry and so much time focusing on things they shouldn't spend time on that there is no balance or meaning to their lives.

At that meal in the refectory, Parseghian also talked about being a team player, telling us how important it is never to let others down. He said that you have to be absolutely determined never to let anybody down. Decades later, I am still struck by how meaningful his exhortation was. In the business world, for example, you are not just performing a service or providing a client relationship; it is more important that you not let somebody down. What you need to ensure is that you are going to give your clients the most you possibly can so that you can help them.

You'd be surprised how much you can get out of helping people. I once knew a man who headed the public relations department at Consolidated Edison, the huge utility company that serves the metropolitan New York area. He subsequently moved from job to job until he found that he was unemployable. Because he was a friend, I spent night after night on the phone with him, advising him on how to get a new job. He finally got one. The irony—and there is nothing wrong with this—was that he never gave me anything back. However, the episode engendered a good feeling in me, a sense of satisfaction that I was able to help someone in distress. Moreover, my ability to write improved. I edited this man's letters to prospective employers and found myself inserting words where I'd never put them before; I was taking more care with the language than I had ever done before.

As a result of all of this, whenever anybody writes me and says, "I'm looking for a job," I always see that person, always respond to him or her. There is a man who came out of the Harvard Business School who had written 400 letters to prospective employers. I was the only person who wrote back to him. Today he's successful in business, and he's become a client of mine. He still remembers that I was the only one who gave him a helping hand when it counted. My advice to power players is that if there is somebody out there who needs a helping hand, give that person an opportunity.

I also learned from Father Hesburgh and friends such as Bill Moyers to assess other people's feelings, not my feelings. This is another important lesson for a power player. You should be able to look outside yourself and say, "Here is how Johnny feels about this, and here is why I should spend some time helping him think through his problem." It's not easy, but once you get to the inner core of what really matters to your client, the solution becomes almost self-evident. Find a way to get to the inner core through a nonoffensive interrogative process; give your clients a sense that you give a damn and that you are not going to compromise them in terms of what they are doing.

As you move up the power ladder, it's important to give back to the institutions and organizations that helped you along the way. I cannot emphasize this point enough; that is why it appears so often throughout this book. You have to remember who your friends are. For example, I went back to Notre Dame and found a way to invest more deeply in the university. I also went to the Ohio State University, where I'd obtained a master's degree, to offer assistance with scholarships and fellowships. In time, people saw me as a guy who was willing to spend time working to make a difference and who had a marketable talent, and they called on me for that talent.

There is a long list of charities in the United States and around the world to which my company sends regular donations. It is a simple way of giving back. There is also a long list of organizations to which we've donated free professional time, what's known in the business as pro bono work. This has become a hallmark of the company, and it is really a good feeling when you do it.

That isn't to say that you should not exercise caution. You have to be very careful about your ethics and make sure you do not compromise your position. Some years ago there was a mayor of Mexico City who approached me with a proposition: He would give me an account worth $6 million in fees in exchange for certain services.

"What kinds of services?" I said.

"You will have to arrange to have some people bring some suitcases across the border every so often," the official said.

And what would be in those suitcases? Cocaine, of course.

"Mr. Mayor, that really isn't something that I can or would do," I said to him.

I'm pretty sure someone else accepted the mayor's offer.

Just as you shouldn't be afraid to reject outrageous requests such as that one in the pursuit of power, you shouldn't be timorous about asking others for help. For example, I turned to my brother, a retired judge, for some advice the other day. His response was extraordinarily generous: He produced an eight-page document that was very well reasoned and very well organized, although it did not offer a conclusion. My brother instinctively understood that I would have to draw my own conclusion and therefore find the solution to the problem I'd discussed with him. He did not have to write the document, but he did, and it was extremely important to me that he did that; it helped guide my decision.

In the power game, the ability to call on people like that is extremely helpful. I once went to a well-known lawyer named Martin Lipton. He didn't give me any business, but he gave me a lot of advice at a time when I was starting my company. Lipton and his wife took my wife and me out to dinner one night. He then sent over several books for me to read and said, "This will really help you launch your new career." Lipton identified several people I should talk to. Lipton is a very bare-knuckled, tough, hard-nosed lawyer, but at the end of the day he is also a very human wonderful person whose spirit of human kindness comes through. Today I see Lipton from time to time, and we have a wonderful relationship. I don't do any business with him, but our relationship is great. There are a lot of people out there who receive acclaim all the time for their professional careers but are deeply humble.

Tami Longaberger is one of those people. She's the chairperson and CEO of a billion-dollar family-owned national direct selling company that her father, David, started in 1973. The Longaberger Company is the nation's premier maker of handcrafted baskets and also offers pottery, wrought iron, fabric accessories, handbags, and specialty foods. Nearly 60,000 independent Longaberger home consultants nationwide sell Longaberger products directly to customers.

Longaberger joined the company in 1984, the same year she received a bachelor of science degree in business administration from Ohio State University. She has led the company through significant growth, product diversification, facilities expansion, and new technologies.

She was named president in 1994 and chief executive officer in 1998.

What impresses me about her are her charm, wit, and humility. She's a great listener, and to observe her working a room is to marvel at her ability to put people at ease.

Her philanthropy and public service are also remarkable. In 1995, Longaberger pledged the company to a broad fund-raising and awareness-building program in a groundbreaking partnership with the American Cancer Society, the Longaberger Company, and the independent Longaberger consultants across the nation. That campaign, Horizon of Hope, has reached 18 million women with breast cancer prevention information and raised more than $12 million for breast cancer research and education.

In recognition of her work, President George W. Bush appointed Longaberger as chair of the National Women's Business Council, a bipartisan federal advisory council that was created to advise and recommend policy to the president, Congress, and the U.S. Small Business Administration on economic issues important to women business owners. She's also been a diplomat representing the United States at United Nations sessions in Geneva.

I sometimes wonder what she has for breakfast. Longaberger is a veritable whirling dervish!

Jack Murofushi is another remarkably giving person. He used to be the CEO of a company called C. Itoh, later to become ITOCHU. He was my client for many years, and we built up a great deal of mutual trust. One day we were at a meeting in which some of the participants said and did embarrassing things. Some of those people were trying to compromise him and take him for a ride. Murofushi was embarrassed and I was embarrassed for him, but he never showed it. He simply smiled. He thanked the people who were around him and walked out of the situation very elegantly. It was a life example for me.

Jack Murofushi—or Murofushi-san, as I called him in the traditional Japanese manner—was also a guy who didn't waste any time. Everything had a point, whether it was leisure or business. He was focused completely on whatever it was. That was a very important lesson for me. He didn't waste an ounce of energy or an ounce of discussion. He just went right for it every single time.

Murofushi was also a man who understood power. Murofushi, more than anybody I've ever met, understood the importance of developing and nurturing a network. He understood how it was important to add people to his network whom he had never met before and to keep in contact with them through letters, e-mails, BlackBerry messages, and phone calls. When Murofushi did that, he always found a way to reach out to somebody that was positive, that drew that person into the conversation, and that endeared him to that person. I'm sure there are thousands of people Murofushi knows around the world because of this networking technique that brought him enormous amounts of power. I hear from him every three or four weeks, and it is always a pointed and interesting communication. His humility is dazzling.

The importance of humility in one's career was brought home to me in a somewhat different fashion in 1968, when I was called up to Columbia University to deal with student riots. Radicals such as Jerry Rubin and Abbie Hoffman stormed into the president's office and occupied it for days. The president, Grayson Kirk, seemed powerless to end the student demonstration.

Kirk turned to the chairman of the erstwhile Irving Trust Company, George A. Murphy, for help. Murphy was quite practiced in dealing with the media, and he decided to hold a press conference. What impressed me most, however, was not his predictably smooth performance but what he had done before meeting with the press. Murphy decided to do a rehearsal. He asked me to throw him the kinds of questions that young reporters were likely to ask, including representatives of the student press. My senior colleagues at Hill & Knowlton blanched. They advised me sotto voce to be extremely careful when tossing questions at Murphy; no hardball, they said.

But Murphy wanted tough questions. He knew that when the real press conference was held, no one would be kind to him. As I threw questions at him, he urged me to get tougher. I was taken with his willingness to be humble with a junior PR executive. In retrospect, it was a clever thing for him to do. The media's questions at the subsequent press conference were far less challenging; in any case, Murphy was well prepared.

I, in contrast, was not as well prepared for the reaction of the man I reported to at the time. His name was J. Robert Cherneff, and he was a former Associated Press reporter who had become vice president of Hill & Knowlton. Cherneff called me into his office after the students had ended their demonstrations. I thought he wanted to praise me for assisting Murphy and generally handling the situation well for the company. Instead, Cherneff wagged his finger at me.

"I'm going to teach you a lesson," he said. "If you ever upstage me again, I'm going to throw your ass out into the street."

I could scarcely believe what I was hearing. I started to shake.

I recovered my composure and then said to him: "Mr. Cherneff, if that is the way you are going to treat me, I don't want to work here. I'm going to go over to Mr. Goss and resign."

My reference was to the company's chairman, Bert C. Goss, who had a reputation for fierce rectitude and also for mentoring up-and-coming professionals. His subordinates were fearful of him. Cherneff certainly was.

"No, don't do that," Cherneff said.

"'Don't do that'?" I said. "But Mr. Cherneff, you just told me I'm going to get my tail booted out of here if I ever do what I should be doing. I was doing the right thing."

"That's right, but you are reporting to me, not to Goss. Don't go out of the line of authority," Cherneff said.

"You just fired me, Mr. Cherneff, and I'm going to go to Mr. Goss," I said.

I went to Goss despite Cherneff's protests. Goss said, "Just go back to your office and relax. I'll take care of it."

I never had a problem with Cherneff after that, and I learned a very subtle lesson: Don't threaten anybody. The best threats are never made: If Cherneff truly had wanted to fire me, he should have gone ahead and done just that without any bluster. In the army they say that if you point the gun, be prepared to pull the trigger. Cherneff was not prepared to pull the trigger. Moreover, he did not possess the humility to let me have my moment in the sun. After all, my handling of the Columbia situation would have reflected well on him.

It is always important in one's professional life to be humble enough to ask for someone's help. George Murphy, tycoon though he was, was smart enough to figure that out. Throughout my career I have benefited immensely by turning to people and asking for assistance. I once wrote a background report and was quite pleased with it but thought I should approach a man named Edward Doherty and ask him to give it a once-over.

"What nationality are you?" Doherty said, somewhat to my surprise.

"I'm of German extraction, but I'm second-generation American," I said.

"That's curious because this doesn't read like English," Doherty said.

He then spent three hours taking the piece apart line by line, sentence by sentence, comma by comma. He showed me the mistakes I had made. That was one of the most constructive lessons of my life. He said, "Here is how you should do this, here is how you should do that." He said, "Here's parallel construction. When you start with an infinitive, always start with an infinitive. When you use a preposition, always use a preposition. Don't split infinitives; do this, do that." He taught me things that I'd never learned before and that in eight years of secondary school and college I was never taught. He taught me how to use action words. He said, "If you are going to start an example like this, why don't you use a word that has some guts to it, some action that gets the message to jump off the page?" I never had been taught that. It was very instructive and helpful.

I've been in the business world long enough to recognize that people, like institutions, serve their purpose. Sometimes even the most benign individuals can seem offhanded to others because those people are distracted. But in professional circles and especially at professional events, it is imperative for a power player to be vigilant. Offense may not be given intentionally, but it often is taken.

Here's an example. The *Financial Times* hosted a breakfast at the "21" Club in Manhattan. The president of the Council on Foreign Relations, Richard N. Haass, and the former president of Harvard University, Lawrence Summers, were the featured speakers. They assessed the significance of the November 2006 election and its meaning for the 2008 presidential vote. Breakfast was laid out in the historic Jack Room, which has hosted many presidents and other dignitaries. Although people were angling to sit at tables near the front, I've always found it more useful to sit at the rear, where you can survey the entire audience and take in the whole scene without having to turn your chair around.

The man next to me was an important lawyer, and I had a piece of valuable information for him. However, he ignored me throughout the breakfast, preferring instead to talk to the man on his other side, an investment banker with the Blackstone Group. At the end of the breakfast I leaned over, put my hand lightly on his forearm, and gave him just a sliver of the information I had. I immediately stood up, walked to an elevator, and got in just before it left. The lawyer didn't make it and found himself squeezed behind a crowd that was using the staircase.

By the time I returned to my office, he had called several times. He wanted to know the rest of my story. I deliberately didn't return his calls until much later that day. I'm sure that the lawyer sweated until we talked again. It had been inappropriate on his part to focus only on the investment banker, particularly since that person clearly was annoyed by the lawyer's incessant self-absorbed chatter. In that equation I was a far more valuable player for him, but he did not recognize it.

Here's another instance of how even top professionals can be insensitive in their workday behavior.

I have a very good friend named Bert Lance, who used to be the head of the Office of Management and Budget in the Carter administration. Bert had a wonderful son, Beverly, who died recently at the age of forty-two. Because Beverly was such a marvelous soul—he was involved in a campaign to rid the Internet of pornography—and because my wife and I have had such a lovely relationship with the Lance family, I told Bert that I wanted to establish a prize in the name of his son. Bert was pleased and suggested a university, and so I called that university's director of development.

His first question was, "How much?"

I said, "How much what?"

"Yeah, how much money are you going to give us?" he said.

If he had not asked me how much but instead had said, "That's really a nice thing to do," I probably would have given more. He wanted to know what the money was. Eventually my wife and I ended up giving a decent amount to establish the prize in honor of Beverly Lance, but I thought that the director had not been smart about the way he handled a call from a potential donor.

Moreover, he told me that he had checked me out on Google, where I have tens of thousands of references.

"Somebody of your caliber can probably get us lots of money or give us insights on how to get lots of money," he said.

"I want to focus on the prize for Beverly Lance," I told him.

He completely forgot the objective of my call, and I kept bringing him back to it. He forgot about my reason for calling in a way that was offensive to me personally.

Contrast that episode with the following one.

I received a telephone call from a man in Maryland who wanted to compliment me on a luncheon speech

I'd helped organize at the Metropolitan Club in New York. The speaker was Hal Vaughan, author of *FDR's 12 Apostles: The Spies Who Paved the Way for the Invasion of North Africa,* a riveting book.

My caller had been among the attendees, and he wanted me to know what a pleasant experience it had been to be at that lunch and hear Vaughan.

"Gosh, this is really great," I said, flattered at the trouble the man had taken to attend the luncheon and then follow up with a call to compliment me for organizing it.

Then he said, "Bob, can you do this for me?"

In a very nice way he made me feel at ease, set me up, and asked me a question. He put me in a position in which if I had said no, I would have been not very nice. Of course, I said I would do it for him. It was all in how he approached it.

If he had approached it originally by saying, "Can you do this?" I automatically would have said, "Let me think about it," but I didn't have a chance to do that. My caller knew exactly what to say and when to say it. Even an old pro like me had to play his power game.

10

Search for Power but Never Forget to Share It

Genuine power players work for a larger cause than consolidating their own power: They empower others.

I OFTEN AM asked by younger colleagues, "What is it like to be with these power people?" My answer always is the same: "It's exciting, it's exhilarating, and when you are adding to what they are doing or being part of their master plan, you say to yourself, 'This is really a great experience. This is really wonderful.'"

Working with people like John Surma, the CEO of U.S. Steel; Serge Tchuruk of France Telecom; Marilyn Carlson Nelson, who runs a private organization, the Carlson Companies, that is bigger than American Express; Alfredo Ambrosetti, one of Europe's top management consultants; and Peter Brabeck, the CEO of Nestlé—is the experience and training of a lifetime.

Are these people important? You bet they are. What stands out about these successful people, for me at least?

Surma works overtime to be with his kids and play hockey.

Tchuruk, one of the most elegant men I've ever met, shares whatever assets he has—his car, his secretarial support, even his laptop—to make one feel more comfortable.

Marilyn Carlson Nelson spends more time helping others develop themselves than anyone I know. "Can you imagine a greater power for good than business?" she asks.

Ambrosetti constantly brings the underprivileged and those in need into his circle to try to help them.

Brabeck, a man of incredible personal strength, will share whatever he has with someone in need if he sees that as being appropriate.

What is it like to be with these men and women of power? With the best of them, it is terrific because they are essentially humble people who understand their own shortcomings. They realize they have a responsibility to help employees, develop their businesses, respond to their shareholders, deal honorably with the press, work with Washington, and increasingly operate on a global basis. They all understand that they are in the spotlight; they can't make a mistake. They all recognize that they have to have somebody they can trust.

I've also found that the best power players have enduring professional values. An example is doing one's homework. Another value is not going into something halfway. Complete and total honesty is also essential. There is so much graft and corruption and corner cutting today, you need to be more vigilant than ever in your professional life.

Once I observed a dubious offer being made to Henry Kaufman, the ranking economist of our time. Kaufman, always generous, listened carefully and then said, "Thank you, but we just don't do it that way here." Kaufman did not insult the man who had made the offer. In fact, I'm not sure that that person knew what had happened. Kaufman just said the most polite no I've ever heard.

Over the years I've had the opportunity to work with and learn from some of the top elected officials of our time, senators like Everett Dirksen, Mike Mansfield, J. William Fulbright, Orrin Hatch, Evan Bayh, and his father, Birch Bayh; governors like Mitch Daniels of Indiana, Jeb Bush of Florida, and Bill Owens of Colorado; and representatives like the late Tillie Fowler of Florida and Chris Shays of Connecticut, among many others.

What marks each of these men and women is total honesty, caring for others, and putting their personal drive in the service of a greater goal. These are exceptional people and models for us all.

Being transparent in their dealings with others is a major characteristic of these power players. Transparency is extremely important in the power game. If people know you are transparent, they will trust you. I'm not saying you have to give everything away, just that you have to ensure that you are do not conceal things that are going to come up later, when someone will say, "Gee, I should have known this."

Power players always look for a higher purpose. Every single person gets up in the morning and says, "How am I going to make enough money to pay the rent and take care of my food bill?" I understand that, but there has to be a higher purpose in terms of what you do in your life.

Society is tough, and a lot of people have a hard time out there. I think we should try to find a way to give back.

For power players, the values of the old world still hold true. They include respecting other people and honoring one's promises. As I mentioned in Chapter 4, on Wall Street there used to be a phrase, "Your word is your bond." Today, with the proliferation of lawyers, it's important that we still have a value like that. It's the ability to be gracious, to be decent. It's the ability to look for a higher purpose. It's the ability to give back. All those things are values that must be inherent in every power player.

Old world manners are everything to me. I think there is nothing like letting a woman go ahead of you on an elevator even if she is a libertarian or a women's rights person. There is nothing like taking your hat off when you greet people. There is nothing like offering to get somebody a drink if that person wants to have a drink. There is nothing like complimenting somebody if it is appropriate without being obsequious. Old world manners make a big difference, and they are part of a power game.

As I look at modern times, I see a lot of hedge fund people, and I say to myself that they want to keep all the money for themselves. That's a big mistake. If they were willing to give some of it back, they'd make a huge statement about themselves. They should find a way to reach out and make society a better place by using the millions and billions they have earned. For the most part, they have not done that.

Sharing your good fortune or power—or empowering others—means that you should recognize how lucky you have been. Whether you give back money, time, insight, energy, or connections, you have to give back because it's the right thing to do. You didn't get there on your own. You got there because a lot of people helped you. A lot of disenfranchised people need to be empowered. As my friends Allan Goodman and Lionel Barber never tire of saying, a genuine power player never thinks about power. I think this comes naturally because of your diligent efforts, because you live by a certain code, because you conduct yourself in a certain way. I think that if you go after power for power's sake, you're making a huge mistake.

You should not walk into a situation saying, "I'm going to be a powerful person, and here's how I'm going to do it." You should walk into a situation and apply the rules because they are the right rules and other rules are wrong. In so doing, you will take a huge step forward. If you appear to be seeking power, trying to make yourself a special person, you will fail along the way.

Rosabeth Moss Kanter, the Arbuckle Professor at Harvard Business School, has long studied power in the boardroom. "Great leaders are purpose-centered, not power-hungry," she says. "They work for a cause larger than themselves and grander even than the particular organization they head. Their legitimacy comes not from the power they wield but from what they do for others."

"They are humble in the face of the magnitude of their tasks, so they temper the inherent self-confidence of accomplished people with glances at the mirror of accountability held up by those they serve," Professor Kanter, the author of sixteen books, says. "They reinforce confidence in the institution as a whole by demonstrating that they are accountable to stakeholders, work with them collaboratively, and empower people inside the organization to speak up, speak the truth, and take the initiative. . . . Their values-based leadership can replace any hunger for power with the deeper satisfaction that comes from a lasting legacy of service to the world."

Sharing your power does not mean diluting it or abdicating your responsibilities. When John Richman was mentoring me while he was the CEO of Kraft, he was empowering me to become a more productive professional and also a more diligent citizen. I observed him and said to myself, "This man is living life the way I would like to live it. He is doing the right thing." The level of humility he possessed was extraordinary. Richman did the right thing and didn't care who saw it. It was wired into him. He had compassion for people; there seemed to be a deep need in him to help the dispossessed. He helped young people at his company. He found ways to use his foundation to give back. He gave back personally in terms of money.

Richman believed that in the final analysis power is ephemeral. You can't take it with you when you enter the great beyond. Warren Buffett, the great investor, showed this understanding when he bequeathed more than $30 billion of his fortune to the William and Melinda Gates Foundation. He was sharing his power not just with the foundation but with the tens of millions of people around the world who will benefit from the better health care, education, and disease control that will be the result of his philanthropy.

I think an important measure of power is that you look for a result. You look for something to happen because you put the plug in the wall; you look for the electricity to flow. You look for something good to occur. I frequently tell people to be very careful. This is a prize you are going to have in your hands for a very short period. Don't abuse it; use it well and you will be successful. However, it's not going to stay with you for your life; it's going to go away.

This means that you must learn to share your power while you have it. Some people think they always will have power all the time, but they won't. It's unfortunate for them because they've got a perception of themselves that is beyond the pale. I meet CEOs who left their jobs and suddenly had no power at all. They think, "I was the CEO of Company X; I still have power," but they don't have power any longer.

When my friend Ari Fleisher was leaving his job as the White House press secretary, I said to him: "Understand that you have power now, but about thirty minutes after you leave the White House, you'll have no power. Thirty-one minutes after that you'll have even less power."

Fleisher, who was as good at his job as any of his predecessors, said: "But I was the White House press secretary."

I said: "People might see you once; people might see you twice; people will take your call because they knew who you were, but unless you can do something for them, they're not going to continue their relationship with you."

Sharing power also means sharing information that will help others understand a situation. For example, when North Korea exploded a nuclear device, I asked William Beecher, a former *New York Times* writer and a Pulitzer Prize winner who specialized in defense issues and now works for my company in Washington, to write an analysis of what that development meant geopolitically. This was at four o'clock in the morning. Beecher, thorough professional that he is, wrote an immensely thoughtful analysis. We wired his essay to all our clients while dawn was still breaking. I know that Beecher's analysis proved useful to many people because some of the best-known names in Washington and around the country asked for an additional briefing.

There used to be a man named Shintaro Abe in Japan. He was the ultimate power broker. He ran the Liberal Democratic Party and served as that country's foreign minister. I used to go to Japan once every two months to brief Abe. We would go to the LDP clubhouse, where hundreds of men and women milled around, much like people in political clubhouses in other parts of the world. Abe and I would go into a private room, and there we would talk for two hours at a time about global issues, about the United States, about technology.

Then Abe would summon his aides one at a time. He would offer a nugget of key information to each one, information that he had gotten privately from me. Abe maintained his power through the use of information. By sharing that power, he in effect consolidated it. It was human technology at its sharpest.

Barney Clark was another skilled practitioner of human technology. When I knew him, he was the head of Columbia Gas, which was based in Delaware. At the end of the day Clark would reach into his desk drawer, bring out a bottle of Jack Daniels, and put it on the desk. You would have a drink with Barney Clark and talk about all kinds of things. He was always gleaning information. He would never disagree with you. If Clark didn't like what you were saying or disagreed with you, he would never say it. He'd say, "Bob, I'm confused." I didn't learn that for some time, but once I learned it, I knew that Clark was saying that he didn't like it, and so I had to adjust my position.

Was Barney Clark sharing his power with me? Yes, in a manner of speaking. He was teaching me to be more disciplined during conversations.

I've been privileged over the years to be in the company of people like Clark and Li Ka-shing, the great Chinese entrepreneur. Li is arguably the man who brought high technology to his part of the world by investing in industries that would facilitate communications and telephony, among other things. He saw me as his window to the West, particularly to New York, because as he often reminded me, about 85 percent of the net worth in the United States is in an area between Boston and Washington.

Li shared an extraordinary insight with me once.

"You Americans, you think that by bringing over your ideas and principles, you are going to change five or ten or fifteen centuries of the way we've been doing things over here in five, ten, or fifteen years," he said. "It's not going to work."

Of course, he was right. The same is true today of the Muslim world. We are not going to persuade Muslims to shed their centuries-old traditions and values. We might even learn from them if we listened and gave back. That would be a real show of power on our part.

Epilogue

IN THE PRECEDING pages I've outlined ideas and reflections about how you as a power player can make your life more productive and positive. The central question should always be this: What are you prepared to do not just in your own life and for your company but in adding value to society? Critical issues are being raised almost daily: global warming, terrorism, the gap between the haves and the have-nots, and the educational divide. Addressing them meaningfully is going to have to be the responsibility of more and more people in societies everywhere, particularly those who possess the power to effect tangible change.

The playbook for obtaining and retaining power is constantly evolving, largely because the technology we increasingly rely on is fungible and is galloping at a pace that's difficult to keep up with. I hope this book will serve as a playbook for people who really want to understand the different uses of power.

My own study of the power game began more than four decades ago. I came out of college in 1965 and did not know what to do. My father said to me, "You have three choices: I can help you get a job at the local department store selling something, maybe selling shoes; you'd be good at that. You can go into the army, or you can go to graduate school."

I said I would go to graduate school and finished the program in nine months. It was very fast, and I got straight A's; it was no problem at all. Then I said to my father, "Now that I've done graduate school, where should I look next?"

His answer: "Well, now you can do three things: Go into the army, get a job here in Columbus, or get a job someplace else."

My dad, who worked for the *Columbus Citizen* newspaper, did not give me any specific advice; he only laid out my options. I decided to take a bus to New York City. On the day I was going to leave, my father sat with me at the kitchen table, and we had a sandwich together.

"I know you are going to do well, but I want you to know that I am here for you if there is ever a problem. Call me if you have a problem, but go do what you have to do now," my father said.

I went to New York and knocked on doors. One of the doors I knocked on was that of Ogilvy & Mather, the ad company. I met a man named Sam Frey, and he offered me a job at $11,000 a year. I said on the spot, "Mr. Frey, I'll take it."

Frey said, "Wait a second. I think there are bunch of guys over at a company called Hill & Knowlton who are from the Midwest like you. You might like them more than the guys here. Why don't you go there?"

"Oh, Mr. Frey, I'll take your job," I said, astonished that he was encouraging me to go to a rival agency.

"Don't worry, the job will still be here tomorrow. Just go talk to these guys," Frey said.

I trundled off to the offices of Hill & Knowlton and talked to a man named Richard Darrow, who had grown up in Mechanicsburg, Ohio; a man named Jim Cassidy, who had grown up in Cincinnati; and John Hill, who had grown up in Shelbyville, Indiana. I found out that they were a lot like me. They had good solid Midwestern values, and they had come to New York to make their way. They offered me a job for $10,000, a thousand bucks less than the Ogilvy job. I took the position immediately.

For many years thereafter, until he died, I took Sam Frey to lunch once a year, thanking him for what he had done for me. I never forgot that he gave me a start in my professional life. That is one reason I like to be a mentor to up-and-coming professionals.

Another reason is that I've always been a student of history. George Santayana famously said that those who do not read history are condemned to repeat it. No power player should be without a copy of the life of Marcus Aurelius, Julius Caesar, Mahatma Gandhi, or Mother Theresa. I'm always happy to produce reading lists for my colleagues, especially the younger ones. My wife and I are always inviting authors, particularly historians, to our home for dinner. You can never extract too many lessons from history.

Then there's contemporary history, or current affairs as it's called. A key lesson I've learned that I like to impart to young people is that in a globalized world you must understand how quickly things move and how important it is to have the right information, ingest it, process it, filter it, and use it in a timely way. Authentic power players share their experience with the next generation of power aspirants.

Those aspirants understand that technology will play an even more significant role in their lives as their careers advance. When it comes to your blog or your PC or your ability to have a personal Web site, ingest pictures on cell phones, or text-message somebody—that understanding is extremely important.

But beyond that you've got to know the fundamental rules of power. Those technological things are really ways to get, ingest, and transfer information, but they do not change the basic rule: You've got to have sound arguments, you've got to use this moment of time, and you've got to use that instant when you appear and do the right thing.

I've found that one rule is paramount: doing the right thing and doing it in a way that makes everybody say that it is the right thing. It's obvious. There are many people who try to cut corners and do something that is unethical and perhaps illegal. Unethical things can be legal things, but those things are wrong.

The rules of the power game apply to both the chief executive and the novice. One is the fundamental Japanese rule of never trying to win 100 percent of everything. You should always make your opponent feel as if he or she got something out of negotiating with you. A lot of people do not do that. They want to beat the other person to the ground. I think the Japanese are very smart. They always give something back and make you feel that you were at least at the party. It should never be "winner take all."

Another rule is that you must have a firm understanding of your objective—what exactly it is that you want to achieve—and the buttons you need to push to get there. Most people don't think about that. They go through life trying to figure out how they are going to get through the next minute, the next hour, or the next half day. The real power player says, "What is my specific objective? What do I want to accomplish here? How do I get that done? How do I use technology to help me get it done?"

Still another power rule that I observe concerns faith. I am a practicing Roman Catholic. The enduring values of belief and prayer help me when dark hours come and I need to set aside my travails. Many readers of this book are likely to be deeply religious; others may not be. For me, religion works. If you accept the idea of God being omnipotent, it does not make any difference which faith you belong to.

So call me old world, call me old-fashioned, or call me a relic from the past, but I believe that the past is prologue. As the Trinidad-born Nobel laureate novelist Sir V. S. Naipaul said, to understand where we are and where we're going, we need to grasp where we've been.

I've been at the power game for a very long time. I've seen some of the rules change, but I've also seen moral values endure the test of time. If you believe, as I do, that everyone's life should have a purpose and that each of us is a custodian of this planet for future generations, welcome to the power game as it should be played.

Let the game begin.

Further Considerations:
Two Concluding Essays
on the Power Game

How the Young Matter
in the Power Game

YOUNG PEOPLE, THE "generation next," those currently 18 to 25 years old,) are very different from the rest of the population. These young people live with and have refined the use of personal computers, cell phones, blogs, the Internet, and much more. They are used to and comfortable with a world of 24/7 in which life changes every few minutes.

Data show that the members of this group are pleased with their lives and optimistic about what lies ahead.

This group understands power, and it wants influence.

A recent Pew Research poll states that a majority of this group says that "getting rich" is their main goal, and large majorities believe that casual sex, binge drinking, illegal drug use, and violence are more prevalent among young people today than was the case twenty years ago.

These young people are very tolerant of social issues—immigration, race, and homosexuality—and are "much more likely to identify with the Democratic Party than was the preceding generation of young people, which could reshape politics in the years ahead."

The Pew data also show the following:

They use technology and the Internet to connect with people in new and distinctive ways. Text messaging, instant messaging, and e-mail keep them in constant contact with friends. About half say they sent or received a text message over the phone in the last day, approximately double the proportion of those age twenty-six to forty.

They are the "Look at Me" generation. Social networking sites like Facebook, MySpace, and MyYearbook allow individuals to post a personal profile complete with photos and descriptions of interests and hobbies. A majority of Gen Nexters have used one of these social networking sites, and more than four in ten have created a personal profile.

Their embrace of new technology has made them uniquely aware of its advantages and disadvantages. They are more likely than are older adults to say that their cybertools make it easier for them to make new friends and help them stay close to old friends and family. However, more than eight in ten acknowledge that these tools "make people lazier."

Clearly, Generation Next is a focus for the future.

Over the last fifteen years more than 100 young people have come through our firm as interns and associates on their way to the future. Look at these five vignettes to see how they feel about power and influence.

A. J. Goodman, Washington, DC

When I think about power and influence, I immediately think about the word *respect*.

In the short time I have been working in the "real world," I have learned that power and influence are not mutually exclusive. On the one hand, an individual can have lots of power but very little influence. On the other hand, an individual can have a great deal of influence but very little power. What ties it all together is respect. In my personal and very limited experience, professional and personal, I have come across two types of leaders: people who lead with respect and people who lead with fear.

People who lead with fear do so through intimidation, and as a result, the level of motivation in their subordinates for getting things done is very low. Their influence on others is such that when their subordinates are told to get tasks done, they want to do that because they fear the inevitable punishment and scorn that would result if they did not accomplish those tasks. In the relationship between the two individuals, there is very little mutual respect: respect for one's leadership, respect for one's ability to fulfill the goals and objectives of the organization, and general respect for each other as human beings.

In contrast, people who lead with respect get entirely different results. Their subordinates voluntarily and willingly follow their lead to fulfill the goals of the organization because they know they will be made to feel a part of something larger than themselves. The influence of these leaders extends to the very core of the people they are leading. They present their subordinates with the opportunity to create something based on their own abilities and intuitions, empowering them; it shows their subordinates that they too have the ability to ascend to their status and position. The obligation to achieve tasks comes from their desire not to let their superiors down and break the bonds of respect and trust.

In trying to articulate what it is I am trying to say, I think of the movie *Braveheart*. In that movie, William Wallace is a Scottish farmer who believes that his country should be free from the rule of the English king, Edward Longshanks. The movie details the various wars into which Wallace leads greater and greater numbers of his countrymen in their quest for freedom. Caught in the middle of the struggle between Wallace and the English king is Robert the Bruce, a Scottish nobleman. In one particularly moving scene, when he's faced with the moral dilemma of siding with Wallace or siding with Longshanks, the Bruce deftly declares the meaning of power and influence and explains why respect is so important. He says passionately that men follow him into battle because if they don't, he throws them off his land and starves their wives and children. However, people follow William Wallace because he passionately believes in the idea that every Scotsman, rich or poor, man or woman, adult or child, should live free to choose his or her own destiny. People respect him and therefore voluntarily follow him into battle and wherever else his crusade may take them.

With respect to technology, in today's modern age, information is power. As the economy continues to outsource most, if not all, manufacturing processes, a new commitment to services-oriented businesses is being made in the United States. After IBM made headlines three years ago by selling off its PC manufacturing unit, it signaled the true start of business transformation in the modern age. The Internet and devices like the

BlackBerry are making it increasingly possible for anyone and everyone to obtain information at a moment's notice. Often, however, this information comes from largely anonymous sources that have no real legitimacy. The issue then becomes one of credibility in that knowing what sources to trust often can be tricky. Suddenly, instead of having concrete written information that was verified and checked regularly because it was printed, anything and everything can sneak into mainstream consciousness and become the day's fodder and topic of conversation, allowing mere rumors to dominate headlines and news. As a result, technology can have a greater and potentially more damaging influence on the minds of people because it comes from anonymous sources of power and authority. As advancements in technology continue to be made, the inherent issue of trust and being able to respect the source from which information and technology comes will be all the more important. Without these two elements in place, there will be no direction for individuals to follow to make the right decisions in their lives.

For some people, power and influence may go hand in hand. For me, however, power has very little influence as long as I cannot and will not respect that power.

Kristina McMenamin, Chicago, Illinois

Many people equate power and influence. In fact, the Merriam-Webster dictionary explains each word in terms of the other. Power is "possession of control, authority, or influence over others," and influence is "the act or power of producing an effect without apparent exertion of force or direct exercise of command." Although the two words are inherently intertwined, in reality few people exhibit both qualities.

Think of our country's leaders. They are powerful. They make the laws that distinguish right actions from wrong ones; in many states they have the ability to condemn a criminal to death as punishment; they send teenagers off to war; and they associate with other powerful people. But how many of our country's leaders are influential in the strictest sense of the term? How many are role models for the nation's youth? How many motivate us to act on causes that matter instead of personal causes like adding to their campaign budgets? How many leaders have enacted change and, more important, encouraged us to enact change?

Whereas power is ubiquitous, influence requires a personal connection.

Think of the public school teachers in our nation's toughest schools. If even one of their students stops dealing drugs or refuses to join a gang because of a teacher, that is influence. A volunteer at a women's shelter who instills a sense of hope and encourages a new mother to get a job and start over—that is influence. An ex-stripper who shares her story and creates a support group for those stuck in the industry so that even one woman can break free—that is influence. These individuals are certainly not powerful, but they are definitely influential.

In today's society, which is run by the powerful and fueled by the media, we are made to believe that influence can come only from above. Technology is slowly reversing that trend. Now anyone can create a Web site and with enough idealism and vision can encourage people to take action. Just the other day I received an e-mail from my roommate's mom asking me to sign an online petition against escalation in Iraq. Youth Noise is a Web site that encourages the nation's youth to take action on poverty and homelessness, enabling students to sign petitions and take part in demonstrations and hunger strikes. The Operation USO Care Package site provides information on how to send Care packages to U.S. troops abroad. All these Web sites and more are influencing the general public to take action. How many politicians can say that they do that?

What this country really needs are powerful people who use their power to influence, to affect people's lives, to encourage us to take action, give back, or speak out. Until that happens, the Internet will have to do.

Anthony Rapacciuolo, Staten Island, New York

These two words—*power* and *influence*—have started wars, defined generations, and completely dictated the outcome of the human race as we know it, yet we as a society fail to ponder their true meaning. There are many theories about why certain individuals have the capacity to exert control over others, but many of them prove to be circular as opposed to linear by nature.

For example, it could be argued that a person who has amassed great wealth will yield power and have a strong influence over others around him or her. Indeed, money is surely a means to an end of power. Anyone with the slightest historical knowledge can recall ancient dynasties and regimes, such as the de Medici family, the Aztecs, and the Incas, that wielded supreme control over society as a result of riches and the ability to hoard the earth's natural resources. Think as far back as Roman emperors or as currently as the president of the United States; all leaders can be traced back to some form of monetary success. Money, then, must be the key to power and influence, correct?

Well, consider this. One of the greatest and most recognized individuals ever to set foot on this earth was born in a stable among wild beasts. He was raised by a poor family and practiced carpentry as his profession. He did not control armies or possess gold, yet those who believe in him far outnumber all the soldiers of all the armies since the beginning of time. His name was Jesus Christ, and his ideologies and beliefs are known worldwide. This single man has had more of an impact on the human race than all the kings in history combined, yet he never sat in a palace. It seems, then, that money cannot be the sole proprietor of power, so let us investigate further.

Niccolò Machiavelli asked, Is it better to be loved or feared? Certainly fear can be equated directly with power. Fear in the hearts of men will make them do unthinkable things, things they would never imagine they had the capacity to do. Fear can rule a country and start revolutions. Recall Adolf Hitler and the Communist Party. Hitler used fear as a vehicle to advance his own agenda, and anyone who stood in his way faced death. It is possible, then, that making others scared of your tyranny is the best way to possess power and influence. By coercing the masses into hysteria, an individual can lead them in almost any direction he or she wishes. Surely, then, fear is the best way to obtain influence.

Not exactly. Think back to the late President Ronald Reagan. This man had his beginnings as an actor, not a politician, yet he ended up heading the most powerful country in the world. No one feared Reagan; everybody liked him and could relate to him on a personal level. I would argue that even those opposed to his political views would admit to his being a nice man in general even if they thought him a terrible leader. The same is not true of Hitler. Reagan gained power by forging agreements and gaining respect, not by threatening to exterminate an entire race. If not fear or love, then there must be some other defining factor that will lead to power.

Technology has in and of itself come to represent power and influence in today's world. Imagine a life without cell phones or e-mail. How could one possibly conduct business without a computer or the Internet? The superpowers of the world all wield nuclear weapons and have the capacity to launch catastrophe with the touch of a button. Our government protects us by bugging our electronic devices to make sure we are not communicating with terrorists or manipulating the board of the New York Stock Exchange to reap illegal cash. In a sense, people living in today's world have devoted a portion of themselves to automation. If someone were to pull the plug, all would be chaos. National security would be breached, our flow of water and electricity would cease, and our health-care facilities would be useless. Finally, then, we can make the assumption that technology is directly proportionate to power and influence.

Although the preceding information is true, if technology dictates ultimate control, Bill Gates would be the president, not George W. Bush. As hard as it is to believe, our society was created and survived without today's modern conveniences. Kingdoms and governments were formed and destroyed before people could comprehend the meaning of the word *nuclear*. Ponder this statement: Society created technology; technology did not create society. Seemingly simple yet profound, that sentence may warrant you to go back and reread it. If you look at the world today, you may think otherwise. It seems that technology has reigned and always will reign supreme, but we know better. Our current technological success is a direct result of centuries that lacked such advances. If we were founded without these devices, we certainly would subsist if they were taken away, and so it wouldn't be fair to say that technology goes hand in hand with power and influence.

Although many more theories exist and all have what seems like irrefutable evidence for being the foundation on which power and influence are built, I will digress to try to identify what I feel is the underlying X factor in all of them. Power and influence would cease to exist if they did not have an agent to exert their control over. In other words, people are victims of their own choices. If you are an introvert or your opinions are easily swayed, you undoubtedly will fall victim to someone else's influence. In retrospect, if you are stolid, determined, and steadfast in your convictions, you have the capacity to use your influence over those people we just discussed.

Ultimately, my premise is that there are no clear-cut indicators that will yield power or influence, whether money, fear, or technology. I suggest that power and influence are simply the manifestation of internal predilections. We all have the ability to be powerful or influential; we must simply master the part of our psyche that gives us the knowledge, capacity, and willpower to do so. All people are created equal, and so it is up to us as individuals to unlock our potential and follow a path toward greatness.

Gina Czark, Chicago, Illinois

It is unfortunate that many young people believe that power is about just money or fame. They consider this their sole motivator and therefore lose sight of how to use their influence. Instead of extending their power outside their offices and into their community, they use it only to benefit themselves through luxury goods and services.

Power to me doesn't equate to money or material items. It's greater than that. Power means knowledge, desire, and having confidence in oneself.

One of the gravest mistakes I see my generation making is believing that it's more powerful to be liked than respected. Power, when wielded correctly, is respected. A powerful leader is one who does not stay the course to please the majority but charts his or her own path and gets successful results.

Technology is one of the easiest ways someone can gain power, although it could be the most dangerous as well. Through the Internet and the eruption of bloggers, a leader easily can exert influence through the posting of his or her ideas and by creating a dialogue with a wide audience. However, I think my generation uses such technology the wrong way. Many blogs are used only for a satirical purpose and therefore risk being more of a joke than a respected means of communication. This can be seen in the emergence of Web sites like MySpace.com and YouTube.com. Instead of using them as a vehicle for intelligent communication and exchange of ideas, many in my generation abuse their purpose.

Those who post to these sites typically are more concerned with reaching a certain number of hits than they are with posting useful information and creating a respected image. The surfacing of these Web sites and blogs has made my generation believe even more that power is about fame and money. The more hits their sites receive, the more notoriety comes with it and the more they are liked.

Power and influence certainly go hand in hand, but without the knowledge and desire to use them for good, they can easily be wasted. If posters to these sites used this extraordinary medium to exert a positive influence and showcase real ideas, their results would be much more successful. But without confidence and foreseeable goals in place, they don't wield much influence and waste their power.

One must be extremely skilled at how to use power and influence. Your power will be more influential if you are respected for the right reasons.

Gianfrancesco Mottola, Rome, Italy

Power and influence are the keys to success. Often they are linked to each other. Who has the power has the influence and vice versa. An individual can have great influence but very little power or a lot of power but very little influence.

When I think about power and influence, I think about respect as well, but in my opinion, power alone doesn't bring respect. Influence alone also can't do it.

For me influence is more important than power, because power doesn't last forever and is arrogant. Influence has a bigger impact, is more diplomatic and elegant, and lasts forever. Influence is an idea or moral statement that can last even over a person's life, even over the centuries. Power ends with life.

Power and influence are important for me. Power and influence are two things that anybody with minimal ambition aspires to have.

When I was twelve years old, I received a book with a dedication from my mother's friend and colleague titled *Power and Influence*. I read it during my university years, and from there I wanted to come to New York to learn directly from the author of the book how to improve my personal power, the ability to communicate and manage information, to handle the clients.

The new technologies are the door to the future because we are in continuous evolution. The Internet and the new ways to communicate are improving day by day and for sure will give people a way to practice power in any field.

Does Your Spouse or Significant Other Make a Difference in the Power Game?

by Jan Dilenschneider

MANY PEOPLE HAVE asked me over the years if a spouse or a significant other makes a difference in the power game.

My answer is: You bet. Those actually are the words of the author of this book. He also happens to be my husband, and hence he should know. After all, we've been married for thirty-seven years and are the parents of two boys, Geoffrey and Peter.

I have seen dozens of examples in which a spouse helps his or her partner attain a new level in that person's profession. I have seen even more cases in which the spouse harms and damages his or her mate, perhaps unintentionally. There is no way people in the power game can separate themselves forever from their spouses. That person is going to come into the light and make an impression sooner or later.

Let me start with four short stories and then offer some basic rules of the game that spouses should consider.

Dr. Glen Nelson was a top executive in Medtronic, one of the storied medical equipment and device companies of our day. Nelson developed some of the most sophisticated medical devices known to relieve pain and suffering. He is an A player in every regard. Nelson also happens to be married to Marilyn Carlson, the CEO of Carlson Companies, the largest travel and leisure company in the world. She's probably the most powerful female executive in the world.

They are the perfect couple. They defer to one another and constantly take the schedules and challenges the other faces into account. Also, they always reach out to others with a level of humility and compassion we should all possess.

But Nelson takes the game up a notch. Marilyn is constantly in the public eye, giving speeches, chairing White House committees, and overseeing hundreds of thousands of Carlson Company workers who attend to customers. Glen Nelson, an A player in his own right, *always* looks for a way to compliment his wife. He does the basics like opening doors and pulling out chairs, but the special ingredient is how he speaks of his wife. Glen talks about his wife in the most positive ways, never crowing about Marilyn but always showing by her example what others might do if they were so inclined.

The result is remarkable. Many recipients of this sort of attention are motivated to achieve a higher professional level; those who witness such personal encouragement often are left breathless.

Then there's Andrea Arnold, a social worker in the Norwalk, Connecticut, school system. She works up close with teenagers who are challenged with some of the difficult problems of the day. Those teenagers know technology, and so Andrea needs to know all about MySpace, how to "I Am," and much more.

Andrea's husband, Bob, is the president of Family Centers Inc., which is based in Greenwich, Connecticut. Family Centers is a social service agency that performs Herculean tasks for the disabled and underprivileged. On any given night you can see Andrea, a person of great significance in her own right, supporting Bob as he works through a gaggle of CEOs. She encourages Family Centers employees, of whom there are more than a hundred, to go to a higher level of accomplishment; she spends time with people who have lost their jobs, are recovering alcoholics, or have lost a husband, wife, son, or daughter to illness.

Andrea Arnold is always there in support. She never upstages; she always adds. She shows humility and graciousness that go far beyond generosity or simply knowing everyone's name. She takes part in Bob Arnold's task, and she adds to it. People around the Arnolds recognize the value they bring to society and become motivated to do more themselves.

The list of spouses who offer sustained support is long in politics. Just think about Betty Ford and the grace with which she handled every element of her life. Reflect on Rosalind Carter and her statements about leaders: "Leaders take us not necessarily where we want to be but where we ought to go." Think about Betsi Shays, who plays a major role in today's Peace Corps. All these women make extraordinary statements for the men in their lives.

It doesn't always work this way.

Here are two examples in which I deliberately mask the names: You will understand why.

Several years ago in Bremen, Germany, a major oil company was holding a celebration at a local drinking club to mark the opening of one of its big refineries. It was a launch event that brought together not just the top executives from the oil companies but also the leadership of the German political and business establishment. Fresh oysters, live lobsters, fine wines and whiskeys, and more were all served. It was quite an affair.

As happens at many such events, there was an extraordinary amount of frivolity.

In any case, halfway through the event, the wife of the new refinery chief walked across the room and told the CEO of the oil company what she thought of him in no uncertain terms. She used four-letter words and examples of how the CEO had damaged and held back her husband's career. She pointed her finger at him and called his wife a harlot. It wasn't a pretty scene.

The CEO of the oil company sat there and took it. He didn't move a muscle. He was surrounded by security men who came forward, but he raised a cautionary hand and let the spouse vent as much as she wanted to. The CEO's wife was shocked. She put her head in her hands and, I believe, wept. Later she told me that she never realized that the individual who had made the accusatory statements actually felt that way.

Those in attendance were all shocked. The spouse's tirade was of such magnitude that it wasn't just the people at the table who were surprised; it was also those sitting at several of the tables around them. You can imagine how the story and the allegations spread through the restaurant.

Finally, the refinery executive was able to bring himself and his wife under control. The two of them walked back to their table, and he offered first a toast (no one took part in it) and then an apology. Again, the CEO of the oil company simply looked at him and accepted what he had to say, and the event moved on, if awkwardly.

The next morning the head of the refinery was looking for a new job.

His office had been locked when he came to work. His secretary had been reassigned.

Guess what happened?

In the second case a top executive at a Fortune 30 company wanted to gain access to a private club in New York where the membership list was blue blood and very difficult to penetrate. It took years to get into that club.

Finally, after letter after letter of endorsement, meeting after meeting to check the individual's bona fides, and the submission of tax and other records to the club to verify his background, the dreaded moment of truth arrived: the final meeting with the membership committee.

The club is a beautiful place near the East River in New York and is one of those establishments where a rude word is never uttered.

The meeting with the committee was at five o'clock in the afternoon. The spouse arrived about thirty minutes ahead of the rest of the people and let the club workers know that her husband was sweating from a workout but soon would be gaining his membership. The workers knew they would have to deal with her from that point on. Many of them had seen it all, but they were shocked by this woman's display.

That was nothing compared to what happened when the meeting started. The woman stood up and said to people who had been members of the club for many years—and they were about as well heeled as anybody in New York—that she would bring into the club her meetings and her friends as well, and they would bring in additional revenues to help the club's bottom line.

She then proceeded to describe the kinds of events and friends she would bring into the club. All this was volunteered, and none of it was asked for. Her husband was shocked, and so were the doyens of the membership committee, who, despite all that had taken place, truly wanted to have her husband in the club.

Like dutiful sentinels, the committee members stood there and listened to the spouse. Finally, the chairman stepped forward and said, "We really appreciate your interest and your views on the club, and we are going to take everything you said and did into consideration."

Two weeks later the husband was visited by an official of the membership committee. He was told that they really wanted him in the club but that his wife would be barred for at least six months and would have to go to a screening by the membership committee again.

Embarrassing? Absolutely!

Today this individual is still not a member of that very fine club. His wife, after three years, has been barred from admission.

So what are some of the basic rules of the game that spouses should think about and follow?

I base my views on contacts I've enjoyed over the years with people like Liz Carpenter, the former press secretary to Lady Bird Johnson; Dick Darrow, Bob's mentor in his early working days; and Jim Cassidy and Carl Lewis, two of the most elegant men I've ever met. I've also distilled ideas from the works of some of the great conversationalists of all time, such as Isaiah Berlin, Winston Churchill, and Denis Diderot, the eighteenth-century French philosopher. Of course, some of the ancients, such as Cicero, the Roman philosopher and politician, are always a source for guidance.

Here are the rules I have come to think are the most important:

- The spouse must make an effort to understand what it is that his or her significant other does. I'm continually amazed at how many people can't relate what their spouses are engaged in. Bob and I hold dinner parties on a monthly basis where we try to engage people in a salon. We discuss an idea or a book or meet an interesting person in public life. We always seat individuals next to people they don't know. All too often, when the man or woman next to them leans over and says, "What does your husband or wife do?" the spouse doesn't seem to know. Such ignorance, even if feigned, does not cast any couple in a good light.
- Know who is important to your spouse and know something about those people. If you are going to do an event, try to understand who the participants are. I've heard my husband tell clients that there are 300 million Americans but probably only 2,000 or 3,000 who make a difference to one's life or profession. If you can define the universe that makes a difference to you, you can focus on that group and on the individuals in that cluster.
- Google these people so that you know them; this is not hard to do, and it is not Machiavellian. In fact, they are probably Googling you. Figure out as much as you can about their lives: which schools they attended, what their publications are, what

their interests are, and more. Such homework will fortify you when you hold conversations with people whom you've never met or know only slightly.

- Always ask other people their views. Liz Carpenter practiced this artfully at dinner party after dinner party. In virtually every state she always used to say to people, How do you feel about this? How do you feel about that? What type of person would you like to have as your guest at this party? She was extraordinarily smart about doing this, and those around the table were flattered when she asked them questions.

- Never interrupt. When people are speaking their piece, they want to say it totally and completely. Anybody who jumps into the middle of an oration from an important person—no matter how good the example or idea he or she wants to express—is generally not well received.

- Always remember people's names, especially their first names. Years ago, Bob and I met Nelson Rockefeller, who told us that he always tried to remember first names because he knew how effective that was in terms of his political life. Well, he was right. I do that as diligently as I can, and I have found that it makes a significant difference. Everyone appreciates the personal touch.

- Listen well. This is a lost art, but if you spend enough time with people and hear what they have to say, you will learn a lot. You also will make people feel that what they are saying is very important, and the reward often is that they will respect you even more.

- Never speak too much. Everybody wants to be heard. G. K. Chesterton, the English essayist, once said that when you are through speaking, just stop. Many people can't do that.
- Never criticize people, either directly or behind their backs. If you have something negative to say, try to find a private forum where you can offer criticism in a constructive manner. Also, assume that whatever you say behind someone's back will get back to that person sooner or later. Many years ago a top executive said to me that one of my closest friends "would sell me out." I said it wouldn't happen. He went on to demonstrate his premise with a man I considered one of my closest friends. He gave that man a secret, and the friend passed it on to several other people within a day.
- Be very serious about grave matters. Life is tough out there, and if you are going to discuss a serious issue, do it in a serious way.
- Always offer to help. People really appreciate it, and few expect it. If your offer is accepted, be sure to keep your word.

Take it from a power player's spouse who's enjoyed a fulfilling career of her own at Estée Lauder, Revlon, and Marshall Fields, among other places: The power game is always about two players—you, of course, but also your spouse. It can be a winning team.

Appendix: The Power Quiz

OKAY, YOU'VE READ the book and digested the lessons. Now it's time to take the next step and use *Power and Influence* to change your life and the lives of those around you and to give back to society.

Here are some questions for you to reflect on. There aren't any conventional answers to these questions. I just want to encourage you to think about the issues we discussed throughout the book: how everything has changed because of technology and how the rules of the power game are changing at warp speed.

After you think about these questions, I invite you to visit my blog at www.dilenschneiderpower.com. Let's start a dialogue. I will respond to all of you.

- What is the difference between power and influence?

- Why is power important to you?
- Why is influence important to you?
- What are three specific steps you intend to take in the next month to inject power and influence into your life?
- If you received a gift in the last six months, did you reply by e-mail, snail mail, or not at all, and why?
- How are you communicating with your family members whom you do not see every day? Is there a better way to do this?
- Who do you know personally that understands how technology can be used to drive power and influence? Can you give any examples?
- How do you use technology to communicate with your spouse or significant other and friends?
- If you acquired the power to transform society, what would your priorities be?
- If you suddenly were stripped of your corporate power, what would you do?

Index